Preparing the Business Plan:

Resources for the Classroom

Justin G. Longenecker
Baylor University

Carlos W. Moore
Baylor University

J. William Petty
Baylor University

SOUTH-WESTERN College Publishing

An International Thomson Publishing Company

Sponsoring Editor: Randy G. Haubner
Developmental Editor: Cinci Stowell
Production Editor: Holly Terry
Internal Design: Rebecca Gray
Cover Design: Joseph M. Devine
Marketing Manager: Stephen E. Momper

GG70ID4

International Thomson Publishing
South-Western College Publishing is an ITP Company. The trademark ITP is used under license.

7 8 9 10 11 12 13 14 15 GP 06 05 04
Printed in the United States of America

ISBN No. 0-538-84475-2

PREFACE

Preparing a business plan may seem like a good idea but a difficult task. In the following pages, we provide information and guidance that will help you get started. The resources are arranged in four brief chapters as follows:

■ *Chapter 1–Introduction to Business Plans*

This chapter gives a short explanation of the plan. It tells who uses such plans and gives a brief review of what is normally included.

■ *Chapter 2–Commentary and Advice of Professionals*

Four brief articles written by experts in entrepreneurship give practical advice and suggestions on writing a plan.

■ *Chapter 3–Developing a Simple Business Plan: Classroom Learning Exercises*

A special project teaches the procedures of plan preparation. We present an example of a basic plan for a very small business. We also describe an assignment and give instructions for creating a plan for another very small business.

■ *Chapter 4–Preparing a Comprehensive Business Plan*

This chapter outlines a more extensive treatment of plan preparation for launching a real business venture of your own. General directions identify the types of questions to be answered and also list other resources that are available. In an academic setting, this might constitute a semester-long project. Sample business plans are included in this chapter.

CONTENTS

1
INTRODUCTION TO BUSINESS PLANS

The first step in starting a business is preparation of a business plan. You can get into business without a plan, but this is risky. You may soon be out of business the same way. A well-designed business plan removes some of the uncertainty and gives the new venture a much better chance of survival.

WHO USES A BUSINESS PLAN?

A business plan is often considered to be a tool to help raise money, and this is indeed one of its purposes in most endeavors. However, this is not its only use, as you can see in Figure 1.

FIGURE 1
USERS OF BUSINESS PLANS

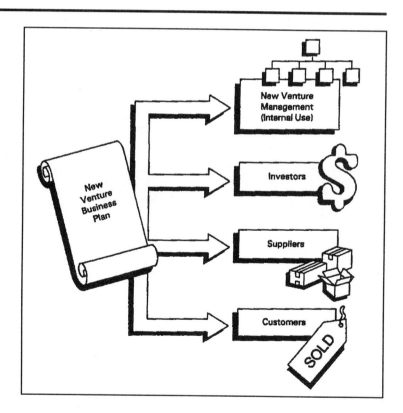

A business plan is basically a blueprint for a new venture. A builder needs appropriate drawings before starting construction. In the same way, an entrepreneur needs basic plans before launching a new firm. Probably the most basic function of a business plan is its use as a guide to entrepreneurial action. Rather than proceeding haphazardly to buy merchandise or raw materials, locate space, and obtain financing, the entrepreneur follows a well-thought-out plan. By using a plan, the owner minimizes unwise commitments and works toward a well-coordinated series of decisions.

If outside funding is needed, a business plan provides documentation that should aid in financing. And, of course, the plan may be useful, as suggested in Figure 1, in dealing with suppliers and customers.

WHAT GOES INTO A BUSINESS PLAN?

Let's assume you understand the value of a business plan and are ready to begin preparing it. Where do you begin? The answer seems simple enough. You include all of the facts and projections concerning the proposed business.

Although that answer describes the broad scope of a plan, it does not give you a starting point. The result may be a conglomeration of facts that disregard some important areas and overemphasize others. The beginner needs a conceptual scheme to identify the important segments of a good business plan. Figure 2 provides such a birdseye view of a plan.

FIGURE 2
OVERVIEW OF A BUSINESS PLAN

Executive Summary:
A one- to three-page overview of the total business plan. Written after the other sections are completed, it highlights their significant points and, ideally, creates enough excitement to motivate the reader to read on.

General Company Description:
Explains the type of company and gives its history if it already exists. Tells whether it is a manufacturing, retail, service, or other type of business. Shows the type of legal organization.

Products and Services Plan:
Describes the product and/or service and points out any unique features. Explains why people will buy the product or service.

Marketing Plan:
Shows who will be your customers and what type of competition you will face. Outlines your marketing strategy and specifies what will give you a competitive edge.

Management Plan:
Identifies the "key players"–the active investors, management team, and directors. Cites the experience and competence they possess.

Operating Plan:
Explains the type of manufacturing or operating system you will use. Describes the facilities, labor, raw materials, and processing requirements.

Financial Plan:
Specifies financial needs and contemplated sources of financing. Presents projections of revenues, costs, and profits.

This figure identifies the basic components of a good business plan. Each section is described in only one or two sentences. In analyzing each of the sections, a prospective entrepreneur develops a carefully-reasoned body of material pertaining to the given topic. Chapters 3 and 4 show some of the more specific questions that must be dealt with in preparing the various parts of this plan.

Figure 3 provides a more detailed outline for each section of a good business plan. When these sections are completed by the entrepreneur, he/she will have a complete but simplified draft of a business plan.

FIGURE 3
OUTLINE OF A SIMPLE BUSINESS PLAN

General Company Description
Name and location
Nature and primary product or service of the business
Current status (startup, buyout, or expansion) and
    history (if applicable)
Legal form of organization

Products and/or Services
Description of products and/or services
Superior features or advantages relative to competing
    products or services
Any available legal protection–patents, copyrights,
    trademarks
Dangers of technical or style obsolescence

Marketing Plan
Analysis of target market and profile of target customer
How customers will be identified and attracted
Selling approach, type of sales force, and distribution
    channels
Types of sales promotion and advertising
Credit and pricing policies

Management Plan
Management-team members and their qualifications
Other investors and/or directors and their qualifications
Outside resource people and their qualifications
Plans for recruiting and training employees

Operating Plan
Operating or manufacturing methods used to produce
    the product or service
Description of operating facilities (location, space,
    equipment)
Quality-control methods to be used
Procedures used to control inventory and operations
Sources of supply and purchasing procedures

Financial Plan
Revenue projections for three years
Expense projections for three years
Needed financial resources
Sources of financing

In developing a full-blown plan for a new venture, the issues shown in Figure 3 merely provide an overall framework. Elaboration of these issues is usually necessary. Chapter 4 shows an exhaustive set of questions that should be considered when developing a comprehensive business plan. The unique nature of the business will determine which are most important.

2
COMMENTARY AND ADVICE FROM PROFESSIONALS

I n this chapter of *Preparing the Business Plan*, four articles are presented to provide valuable insights into the development of a business plan. The articles, originally appearing in business periodicals, are authored by experts who bring unique perspectives to the task.

The first article, "How to Write a Business Plan," is written by J. Tol Broome, Jr., a Senior Vice President of Banker's Trust in Greensboro, NC. His focus is the use of the plan to obtain financing. He provides several suggestions for writing a plan and also identifies several mistakes to avoid.

The second article, by Donald F. Kuratko, Director of the Entrepreneur Program at Ball State University, provides a comprehensive explanation of a business plan. This article, appropriately titled "Demystifying the Business Plan Process: An Introductory Guide," will give you a basic overview of the plan's components and offer helpful hints for effective writing.

The third article, "A Good Plan Is Key To Business Success," is authored by journalist Shelly Branch. Taken from *Black Enterprise*, this article discusses the business plan from the perspective of a minority entrepreneur, but it is broadly applicable to plan preparation. It gives a quick look at some of the most critical components of the business plan — understanding the market, financials, and the management team.

The last article, "The Business Plan That Gets the Loan," is taken from *Working Woman*. In it, Louise Washer provides a woman's slant on writing a business plan. She includes a detailed account of the real-life adventures of two female entrepreneurs as they developed their business plan and launched their business.

HOW TO WRITE A BUSINESS PLAN

By J. Tol Broome Jr.

Your loan has been approved. Those words are music to the ears of the business owner seeking bank financing for a new venture or expansion of an existing company. But the music won't play if the owner hasn't submitted a well-conceived business plan.

It's not a daunting task, however, to make sure a business plan contains the elements that will win a positive response from a lender. In fact, there are even certain banker "hot buttons" that can be pushed in preparing a business plan — details that might make the difference between approval and denial of a loan application.

Following are the basic points of an effective business plan.

Quality vs. Quantity

In evaluating plans, most bankers do not abide by the credo of "the bigger, the better." Succinctness is critical in preparing an effective plan that will appeal to the lender.

"Our bank is big on bullets of information," says Bill Holt, a vice president with Wachovia Bank of North Carolina, which is based in Winston-Salem and is one of the leading small-business lenders in the Southeast. Holt, who heads the Reidsville, N.C., office, says: "We are looking for a good, concise summary, not a thesis. In fact, we prefer to see the facts presented one by one rather than in a paragraph format. We are making a factual decision, so we want facts, not fluff."

For instance, in providing industry background to a personal-computer wholesaler, a concise page or two of facts pertaining specifically to that segment of the PC market and the target market area will be much more effective than a 15-page dissertation on the entire computer industry.

According to Len Ferro, director of entrepreneurial services for Ernst & Young's Greensboro, N.C., office, the average business plan gets 15 minutes of review. "So it's important to make your words count in the plan," he says.

The most critical section of the narrative content may be the executive summary. "First impressions are critical," says Holt. "The executive summary provides the lender with the first impression of the business." The summary should not be used simply to introduce the business idea; it should provide a synopsis of the key reasons why the idea will

work. A well-organized executive summary will usually entice the banker to read on; a poorly conceived summary probably will lead the loan officer to move on to the next request.

Seeking Outside Help

Many entrepreneurs try to prepare a business plan themselves; they think that seeking outside help would demonstrate weakness to the banker. On the contrary, in the eyes of most lenders, a borrower who seeks input and counsel from knowledgeable sources generally is seen as having put his or her idea to the test before going to the bank.

Moreover, seeking third-party help may not be costly for the borrower. Some CPA firms offer low-cost or even free help in preparing business plans. In addition, free counseling services are available in many communities through the Service Corps of Retired Executives (SCORE) and Small Business Development Centers, two programs sponsored by the U.S. Small Business Administration. Some colleges, including community colleges, also have entrepreneurial and other small-business assistance programs.

"A couple of years ago, I had a plastics company apply for a loan," says Holt. "All the owner knew was that he wanted a line of credit, but he didn't know how much or why he needed it.

"We recommended that he seek advice from a local small-business incubator. He came back with a business plan that included background on the business, personal information on the principals, and projections reflecting how the loan would be repaid, and we made the loan."

A business plan is no place for humility. The lender wants to know the experience of the owner and other key personnel, particularly their experience in the industry in which the venture will operate. A person who has 15 years of experience in book retailing and seeks a loan to open a bookstore will have a better chance of getting approved than a person starting a bookstore with 15 years of experience in the restaurant business.

The backgrounds of the key people can be presented in a resume format.

Addressing The Pitfalls

Bankers are notoriously pessimistic. Consequently, if the business owner fails to address the potential hurdles to success, the loan officer will do it for him or her.

"A business plan that is filled only with good news immediately sends up a red flag for me," says Charles Cannaday, the chief lending officer for First South Bank, a small, community bank in Burlington, N.C., that deals exclusively with small to medium-sized businesses.

"Not considering the potential problem areas in the plan tells me that the prospective borrower really hasn't thought through the idea," says Cannaday. "If he hasn't been thorough enough to address the pitfalls, then why should I take the chance of making the loan?"

According to Ernst & Young's Ferro, many business owners have only a Plan A: "This product or service is so great that no one can afford not to have it." They often ignore the hard questions that must be asked. Among them:

■ What happens if my prospective customers don't catch on to the need as quickly as I think they will?

■ What if they catch on too fast?

■ What if they aren't willing to pay my price?

■ What if the product costs more to produce than I had planned?

■ What if a competitor with deeper pockets and a more established reputation enters the market?

Addressing the prospective pitfalls can be quite tricky. Omission of possible hurdles suggests that the loan applicant has unrealistic expectations. On the other hand, the business owner can't devote the entire plan to the potential obstacles.

A delicate balance must be achieved in which the business owner explains why the idea will work even if things don't proceed as planned. In effect, the owner must be able to call the proverbial glass of water both half full and half empty.

The Repayment Question

The key question for every loan officer is: How will the bank be repaid? In nearly every small or medium-sized business endeavor, the answer depends on cash flow. So, what's the bottom line? Prospective profits. Hence, financial projections in the plan are critical.

"Frankly, I usually start with the projections and work backwards," says Cannaday of First South Bank. "If the projections reflect an insufficient cash-flow level or are unrealistic, there's no need for me to waste my time or the borrower's by reading and discussing the rest of the plan."

The financial section is where many a business plan goes awry. Bankers are looking for no-nonsense numbers that are adequately backed up by reasonable assumptions. The problem is that many business owners provide only the best-case set of projections reflecting nearly impossible marks for sales and net income.

"When the projections are too high, I lose confidence in the owner," says Brent Priddy, a business-service officer with BB&T, a bank headquartered in Wilson, N.C., that focuses most of its lending efforts on small to medium-sized businesses in the Carolinas. "Unrealistic projections lead me to begin to wonder if the borrower is still trying to convince himself about the viability of his business."

Like most loan officers, Priddy, who is based in Greensboro, says he prefers to see three different sets of projections—best-case, worst-case, and most-likely-case scenarios. This demonstrates to the banker that the owner has considered all possible risks.

Looking at three different cash-flow scenarios also will help the entrepreneur better understand his or her working capital needs. Rapid sales growth (even under very profitable conditions) can affect those needs as much as extended losses. And one of the cardinal sins of starting or expanding a business is underestimating the need for working capital.

"I like to see a borrower complete a projected balance sheet as well as an income statement," says Cannaday. "Without doing a pro forma balance sheet, there is no way to really analyze the effects of growth on working capital. When a company experiences sales growth, trading assets will also increase. It is critical that the business owner understand this correlation before he proceeds with the endeavor."

One banker provided a prime example of the need to scrutinize potential working-capital shortfalls. His bank had lent money to an entrepreneur to open a pizza franchise. When the parent company became bankrupt, the franchise owner (who had planned for the worst) was prepared. He had set aside a large cash reserve in case circumstances turned against the business. Consequently, he was able to take the three months necessary to revamp the facility into an upscale pizza restaurant without losing any of his key employees.

Two years later, the revitalized concept has proven successful. Revenues have grown to a level that is more than sufficient to meet expenses and service debt, and the owner is franchising his idea in a venture that promises to be lucrative.

Along with the business plan, bankers like to see the entrepreneur submit a specific loan request. They usually prefer that the owner list not only a requested amount but also the proposed loan components, such as purpose, term, interest rate, and collateral. The terms may not be accepted as proposed, but they will at least provide a starting point for negotiation.

By including a complete loan proposal with the plan, the owner demonstrates to the lender that he or she understands not just the need for financing but also why the funds are needed to make the venture work.

Bankers agree that preparation of a business plan is essential to any loan request. As the saying goes, those who fail to plan, plan to fail.

Mistakes to Avoid in Drafting a Plan

Here are errors in business-plan preparation that almost certainly will result in denial of a loan application by a bank:

■ Submitting a "rough copy," perhaps with coffee stains on the pages and crossed-out words in the text, tells the banker that the owner doesn't take his idea seriously.

■ Outdated historical financial information or industry comparisons will leave doubts about the entrepreneur's planning abilities.

■ Unsubstantiated assumptions can hurt a business plan; the business owner must be prepared to explain the "whys" of every point in the plan.

■ Too much "blue sky" — a failure to consider prospective pitfalls — will lead the banker to conclude that the idea is not realistic.

■ A lack of understanding of the financial information is a drawback. Even if an outside source is used to prepare the projections, the owner must fully comprehend the information.

■ Absence of any consideration of outside influences is a gap in a business plan. The owner needs to discuss the potential impact of competitive factors as well as the economic environment prevalent at the time of the request.

■ No indication that the owner has anything at stake in the venture is a particular problem. The lender will expect the entrepreneur to have some equity capital invested in the business.

■ Unwillingness to personally guarantee any loans raises a question: If the business owner isn't willing to stand behind his or her company, then why should the bank?

■ Introducing the plan with a demand for unrealistic loan terms is a mistake. The lender wants to find out about the viability of the business before discussing loan terms.

■ Too much focus on collateral is a problem in a business plan. Even for a cash-secured loan, the banker is looking toward projected profits for repayment of the loan. The emphasis should be on cash flow.

Source: *Reprinted by permission,* Nation's Business, *February 1993. Copyright 1993, U.S. Chamber of Commerce.*

DEMYSTIFYING THE BUSINESS PLAN PROCESS: AN INTRODUCTORY GUIDE

By Donald F Kuratko, Ph.D.

The world does not need another article on business plans. If you have decided to write a business plan, you probably already know that there are too many books, tapes, videos, software programs, and seminars already. It has been called the "business plan jungle" because unsuspecting entrepreneurs have been known to get lost in the rows of resources at their local bookstore, never to be heard from again.

How is this article different? It is designed to be your starting point — the first source to read before wading through the stacks of lengthier resources. By providing an overview of the standard sources, and the insights I have gained by working with literally hundreds of plans, I hope to help you determine whether you should write a business plan. And, if you decide to proceed, the information given here will help you take the next step.

What Is a Business Plan?

A business plan:
- Describes every aspect of a particular business.
- Includes a marketing plan.
- Clarifies and outlines financial needs.
- Identifies potential obstacles and alternative solutions.
- Establishes milestones for continuous and timely evaluation.
- Serves as a communication tool for all financial and professional sources.

The business plan is the major tool used in guiding the formation of the venture, as well as the primary document in managing it.

But it is also more than a written document — it is a process that starts when entrepreneurs begin to gather information and then continues as projections are made, implemented, measured, and updated. It is an *on-going* process.

The Benefits

Financing. Venture capitalists and most banks require business plans. Generally, when our national economy declines, it becomes harder to obtain financing, and financiers increase their demands for documentation. Many entrepreneurs say that they wrote a business plan because their bankers or venture capitalists required them to.

Increased knowledge. But many of these same entrepreneurs say that just as important as getting the financing was the process of actually having to put the plan together. Writing the plan forced them to view the business critically, objectively, and thoroughly.

Prevent poor investments. Business plans help entrepreneurs avoid projects that are poor investments. As Joseph Mancuso says In *How to Write a Winning Business Plan*, "If your proposed venture is marginal at best, the business plan will show you why and may help you avoid paying the high tuition of business failure. It is far cheaper not to begin an ill-fated business than to learn by experience what your business plan could have taught you at a cost of several hours of concentrated work."

Planning. Business plans force you to plan. Because all aspects of the business venture must be addressed in the plan, the entrepreneur develops and examines operating strategies and expected results. Goals and objectives are quantified, so that the entrepreneur can compare forecasts with actual results. This type of planning can help keep you on track.

As a final note about the benefits, let's acknowledge that entrepreneurs who do all or most of the work themselves are the ones who tend to benefit most from the plans. Those who delegate this job tend to gain the least.

The Components

Here is a brief description of the ten components of a business plan:

Executive summary. This is the most important section because it has to convince the reader that the business will succeed. In no more than three pages, you should summarize the highlights of the rest of the plan.

The Executive Summary must be able to stand on its own. It is not simply an introduction to the rest of the business plan. Investors who review a lot of business plans may read only the Executive Summary. If the Executive Summary is not successful in gaining the investor's confidence, the plan will be rejected and will never be read in its entirety.

This section should discuss who will purchase the product or service, how much money is required, and what the payback is expected to be. You should also explain why you are uniquely qualified and skilled in managing the business.

Because this section summarizes the plan, it is often best to write this section last.

Description of the business. This section should provide background information about your industry, a history of your company, and a general description of your new product or service.

Your product or service should be described in terms of its unique qualities and value to consumers.

Specific short-term and long-term objectives must be defined. You should clearly state what sales, market share, and profitability objectives you want your business to achieve.

Marketing. There are two major parts to the marketing section. The first is research and analysis. Here, you should explain who will buy the product or service — or, in other words, identify your target market. Measure your market size and trends, and estimate the market share you expect to capture. Be sure to include support for your sales projections. For example, if your figures are based on published marketing research data, be sure to cite the source. Do your best to make realistic and credible projections.

Describe your competition in considerable detail, identifying their strengths and weaknesses. Finally, explain how you will be better than your competitors.

The second part is your marketing plan. This critical section should include your market strategy, sales and distribution, pricing, advertising, promotion, and public awareness.

Demonstrate how your pricing strategy will result in a profit. Identify your advertising plans, and include cost estimates to validate the proposed strategy.

Research, design, and development. This section includes developmental research leading to the design of the product. Industrial design is an art form that has successfully found its way into business, and it should not be neglected. Technical research results should be evaluated.

Include the costs of research, testing, and development. Explain carefully what has already been accomplished (e.g., prototype development, lab testing, early development.)

And finally, mention any research or technical assistance that has been provided for you.

Manufacturing. Explain the process steps to be used in producing your product or service. A simple flowchart is often used to show how a product will be assembled.

This section should also describe the advantages of your location in terms of zoning, tax laws, wage rates, labor availability, proximity to suppliers and transportation systems.

Outline also the requirements and costs of your production facilities and your equipment. (Be careful — too many entrepreneurs underestimate this part.)

Organization. Start by describing the management team, their unique qualifications, and how you will compensate them (including salaries, employment agreements, stock purchase plans, levels of ownership and other considerations). Discuss how your organization will be structured and consider including a diagram illustrating who will report to whom.

Also include a discussion of the potential contribution of the board of directors, advisers, and consultants.

Finally, carefully describe the legal structure of your venture (i.e., sole proprietorship, partnership, or corporation).

Critical risks. Discuss potential risks before investors point them out. Here are some examples: price-cutting by competitors, potentially unfavorable industry-wide trends, design or manufacturing costs that could exceed estimates, sales projections that are not achieved, production development schedules that are not met, difficulties or long lead times in procuring parts or raw materials, and greater-than-expected innovation and development costs to keep pace with new competition.

Outside consultants can often help identify risks and recommend alternative courses of action.

Your main objective is to show that you can anticipate and control (to a reasonable degree) your risks.

Financial. This section of the business plan will be closely scrutinized by potential investors, so it's imperative that you give it the attention it deserves. Three key financial statements must be presented: a balance sheet, an income statement, and a cash flow statement. These statements typically cover a three-year period. Be sure you state all the assumptions you made when calculating the figures.

Determine the stages where your business will require external financing and identify the expected financing sources (both debt and equity sources). Also, clearly show what return on investment these sources will achieve by investing in your business. The final item to include is a break-even chart. This chart should show what level of sales will be required to cover all costs.

If the work is done well, the financial statements should represent the actual financial achievements expected from the business plan. They also provide a standard by which to measure the actual results of operating the enterprise. They become a very valuable tool for managing and controlling the business in the first few years.

Milestone schedule. This is an important segment of the business plan because it requires determining what tasks must be accomplished in order to achieve your objectives. Milestones and deadlines should be established and monitored while the venture is in progress. Each milestone is related to all the others and together they comprise a network of the entire project.

It may be helpful to summarize this section in a chart.

Appendix. This section includes important background information that was not included in the other sections. This is where you would put such items as: resumes of the management team, names of references and advisers, drawings, documents, agreements, and any materials that support the plan. You may also wish to add a bibliography of the sources you drew information from.

Writing Your Plan

The best way to start your plan is to find out what information you will need to acquire. The preceding outline is a good sketch; now go after complete information.

In my experience, the two most common stumbling blocks when writing business plans are: finding the information and writing the document.

Acquiring your information will probably be the most time-consuming part of the business plan process. Here is a brief sampling of the types of places that may have the kind of information you will need.

Data sources for your business plan
Sources of internal data
■ Accounting records
■ Marketing studies
■ Customer complaint files
■ Sales records
■ Other company records

Sources of external data
General guides (These guides provide direction on where to go to find data on a particular topic.)
■ American Statistics Index
■ Business Information Sources
■ Consultants and Consulting Organizations Directory
■ Directories in Print
■ Directory of Industry Data Sources
■ Directory of On-Line Databases
■ Encyclopedia of Associations
■ Encyclopedia of Business Information Sources

■ Small Business Sourcebook
■ Statistical Reference Index

Indexes to books and articles:
■ Applied Technology and Sciences Index
■ Books in Print
■ Business Periodicals Index
■ Computer Database Information Searches
■ Reader's Guide to Periodical Literature
■ Standard Periodical Directory
■ Wall Street Journal Index

Government publications:
■ Census Reports (agriculture, construction, housing, manufacturers, mineral industries, population, retail trade, service industries, transportation, wholesale trade)
■ County and City Data Book
■ County Business Patterns
■ Economic Indicators
■ Guide to Foreign Trade Statistics
■ Guide to Industrial Statistics
■ U.S. Industrial Outlook

Organizations and people:
■ American Marketing Association
■ Friends, relatives, and other small-business owners
■ Librarians
■ Local Chamber of Commerce Offices
■ Local and regional newspapers
■ Marketing research firms
■ Small Business Development Centers (SBDCs)
■ State, local, and federal government offices
■ Trade associations
■ Universities

Drawbacks and limitations. If business plans are so great, how come a lot of old, successful businesses don't have one?

Some business owners succeed without this tool because they are geniuses, they are lucky, or because they have an incredibly great product or service. What you don't see are all the businesses that didn't make it but might have done better if they had put a plan together.

Many established business owners, quite frankly, could benefit from going through the process. I know of one 110-year-old business that decided to write a business plan because its owners needed to re-define their target markets. For three months, they met weekly with an outside consultant, and they said they literally "turned the business inside out." They're pleased with the results. Two years after going through the process, their sales are up 80 percent and their profits are up 300 percent.

Perhaps the main reason that some businesses don't have a business plan is that this type of planning goes against the nature or personality of many entrepreneurs. They would much rather be "doing something" than planning, projecting, and calculating. The thought of spending three months (or even three full days) doing research makes them uneasy.

Finally, some entrepreneurs may feel skeptical about the value of a plan that is, after all, based upon estimates. If you are writing a plan for a new business or a new product, all of your calculations will, of course, be guesswork. The value of your "guesswork" depends upon what you are basing your assumptions on. Your research needs to be thorough, accurate, and applicable to your own situation.

Even though business plans should take risks into account, it is impossible to identify all the unforeseen circumstances that may arise. Who can predict natural disasters or sudden serious illnesses? Insurance can help cover some losses, but it cannot ever put you back in exactly the same position you were in before.

And it can be hard to know when you have satisfactorily answered such questions as, "Who are my customers?" and, "How much of my product will they buy in a given period of time?" A common limitation of all of the resources I've listed is that they are not interactive. In other words, they cannot ask you questions like "Have you considered this as a possible market? Have you thought about this drawback?" That's why I highly recommend that you talk with someone about your plan before you consider it finished.

Doing a business plan won't guarantee success. It won't remove risk or uncertainty. And it won't always result in financing.

But business plans can help entrepreneurs make informed decisions. For that reason alone, they almost always prove to be a good investment in terms of time and effort.

A Common Stumbling Block: The Writing Process

Your desk is covered with pieces of information that you want to put into your business plan. You've had your coffee. Your phone is off the hook. But you spend the next fifteen minutes staring out the window...unable to get going.

You're not alone. Most people experience some form of writer's block when faced with a particularly important or large-scale job.

Why? Most researchers who study the act of writing currently believe that many of our writing problems are caused by our approach. They say that all writers — whether they are conscious of it or not — go through this five-stage process when they write: pre-writing, writing, revising, editing, and proofreading. The majority of writing problems are caused, the researchers say, when the writer tries to do all of the steps at once. Let's take a closer look at each of these steps:

Pre-writing. This is the stage where you decide what you're going to say. You may write or review your notes, assemble facts, organize your thoughts, establish your goals, or draft an outline. The more you have to say, the more important this stage is. Generally, the more time you spend here, the less time you will spend in the revising stage.

Writing. After you know in broad terms what you need to say, you can start saying it. This is the stage where you just get it down. Resist the temptation to try to say everything perfectly. Don't correct grammar or punctuation. Don't stop after every sentence to critique yourself. Just keep going.

Revising. When you're done, you can start revising for clarity. Re-work your sentences until you are sure that your reader will understand them.

Then, take a break from the project. At the very least, return a phone call or stand up and stretch. The next stage will require you to switch gears dramatically, and it will be much easier if you approach it from a fresh perspective.

Editing. This is the most crucial — and most difficult — stage of the writing process. At this point, you should take a very objective look at your business plan and ask yourself:
■ Does it do what it should do?
■ Is it convincing?
■ Do I need to include more information? Less?
■ Have I supported all of my most important statements?
■ Is it well-organized?

■ Is it readable?
■ Is the tone appropriate? Is the style appropriate?

Proofreading. All that is left to do now is to look for typographical errors, minor grammatical errors, and to make sure that the business plan is spaced correctly on the page. It helps if someone else can take a look. Keep in mind that minor errors could undermine the impact of the whole business plan.

The most important applications of the process approach are: Don't correct yourself while you write, and don't wait for "the perfect opening sentence" to come to you.

Speaking from my own experience as a professional writer (who hates to write), this process approach makes a lot of sense. I consciously go through the steps about 90 percent of the time. While I taught this at University of Wisconsin-Milwaukee, about 75 percent of my students said that this approach saved them time and was especially helpful when they had tight deadlines.

— Catherine Stover, Editor

A Business Plan Checklist: Key Questions to Answer

I. Executive Summary
a. Why will the business succeed?
b. What do you want to start (or change)?
c. How much money is required?
d. What is the return on the investment?
e. Why is the venture a good risk?

II. Business Description
a. What type of business are you planning?
b. What products or services will you sell?
c. What type of opportunity is it (new, part-time, expansion, seasonal, year-round)?
d. Why does it promise to be successful?
e. What is the growth potential?
f. How is it unique?

III. Marketing
a. Who are your potential customers?
b. How large is the market?
c. Who are your competitors? How are their businesses positioned?
d. What market share do you anticipate?
e. How will you price your product or service?
f. What advertising and promotional strategies will you use?

IV. Research, Design, and Development
a. Have you carefully described your design or development?
b. What technical assistance have you received?
c. What research needs do you anticipate?
d. Are the costs involved in research and design reasonable?

V. Manufacturing
a. Where will the business be located? Why?
b. What steps are required to produce your product or service?
c. What are your needs for production (e.g., facilities and equipment)?
d. Who will be your suppliers?
e. What type of transportation is available?
f. What is the supply of available labor?
g. What will it cost to produce your product or service?

VI. Organization
a. Who will manage the business?
b. What qualifications do you have?
c. How many employees will you need? What will they do?
d. How will you structure your organization?
e. What are your plans for employee salaries, wages, and benefits?
f. What consultants or specialists will you need? How will you use them?
g. What legal form of ownership will you choose? Why?
h. What licenses and permits will you need?

VII. Critical Risks
a. What potential problems could arise?
b. How likely are they?
c. How do you plan to manage these potential problems?

VIII. Financial
a. What is your total estimated business income for the first year? Monthly for the first year? Quarterly for the second and third years?
b. What will it cost you to open the business?
c. What will your personal monthly financial needs be?
d. What sales volume will you need in order to make a profit during the first three years?
e. What will be the break-even point?
f. What will be your projected assets, liabilities, and net worth on the day before you expect to open?
g. What are your total financial needs?
h. What are your potential funding sources? How will you spend it?
i. How will the loans be secured?

IX. Milestone Schedule
a. What timing have you projected for this project?
b. How have you set your objectives?
c. Have you set up your deadlines for each stage of your venture?
d. Is there a relationship between events in this venture?

X. Appendix
a. Have you included all important documents, drawings, agreements, and references?

Source: Reprinted with permission from the Small Business Forum, *Winter 1990/1991. Copyright 1990 by the Regents of the University of Wisconsin System.*

A GOOD PLAN IS KEY TO BUSINESS SUCCESS

By Shelly Branch

Given the chance, any entrepreneur will wax rhapsodic about his or her latest venture.

But it's work, not words, that turns an idea into reality. And the proof of a well-researched and carefully designed idea is its ability to attract capital. The goal is to enlist willing investors, whether they are commercial lenders (such as banks), family members, business "angels," or minority enterprise small business investment companies (MESBICs).

However, money is tight. This year, Needham, a Massachusetts-based Venture Economics Publishing Co., reported that small companies got 60% less from venture-capital sources than in 1990. And a recent study done by the American Institute of Certified Public Accountants showed that 10% of community banks are routinely turning down qualified borrowers.

Thus, the importance of a comprehensive, attractive business plan is clear.

Unfortunately, many entrepreneurs view writing a plan as a chore and not an essential function of business survival. But, says Joseph Mancuso, president of the Center for Entrepreneurial Management in New York City, "Who'd take a road trip without consulting a map? The same principle applies in business — you need direction."

Don't worry. There is plenty of help available. Just remember, there are five basic components of a winning business plan.

1. The Executive Summary

In business, first impressions count. So your one- to three-page opener should be an aggressive attempt to sell your readers. "The summary should give people the feeling that this is a venture that can be profitable," says Nancy Flake, director of Howard University's Small Business Development Center. "It must entice the reader to read on."

As the preface to your plan, the summary outlines the ways, means and goals of your business. Start out with clear descriptions of your product, customers, and suppliers and address any obvious concerns. You need to identify your niche and state any specific advantages you hold over the competition.

Next, lay out your company's primary goals and achievements. If your start-up seems able to turn a profit in 18 months, say so and refer to financial projections that back you up. Existing companies should parade their most impressive achievements, including any initial goals that were exceeded or industry awards bestowed.

Finally, give a rundown of management, history, and finances. Who are the key decision-makers? What are their qualifications? How long has the company been in business? How has it performed? These are subjects you'll also return to in the plan, but it's important to touch on them briefly. Also, be clear about your objectives. If the plan's goal is to obtain financing, "say how much right up front," advises Flake. "Then the plan itself will back up how you've arrived at that figure and what you'll do with those dollars."

2. Understanding the Market

To prove you've got a firm grasp of your territory, your plan must size up the market. Who are your customers, and why will they be attracted to your product or service? What's your price and how did you figure it? Though the answers to these questions might seem obvious to you, they must be presented as the product of careful research. "Market analysis provides evidence that you've got a workable idea," sums up Thomas Clark, management professor at Xavier University in Cincinnati. "It shows that there's a good match between what you're selling and the customers' needs."

Your market overview should include sections on your target market's size and demographics, as well as your chosen industry's competitiveness and health. Gathering this information means hard work. And since professional research firms charge upwards of $2,000 per analysis, chances are you'll do it yourself. Still, you can give this section depth by using easily tapped resources.

A good place to start is at the local library. You can peruse the Department of Commerce's *U.S. Industrial Outlook* — which contains economic data and forecasts on 350 industries — and use that data in your own projections for growth and profitability.

Demographic information is available from both local and regional census reports. Chambers of commerce help identify your competition, while state planning commissions can tell you about any commercial developments headed for your area. Dig even further by contacting trade associations in your field. Most hold annual conventions or trade shows, where you'll get the lowdown on industry trends. And don't forget to investigate regional chapters. They may offer price schedules for your industry's products and services and provide great networking opportunities.

Thoughtful research is what set Harvey Hamlett's plan apart from the pack. In 1987, the Atlanta entrepreneur spent months canvassing leads on his plan to put electronic video ads over phone booths. Inquiries at several companies led him to a study on video kiosks; it was packed with favorable data relevant to his own plan. But the clincher was a feasibility study on the marriage of advertising and pay telephones: That gem contained proof that pay phones could deliver the kind of audiences advertisers kill for. "I used every shred of research, every number I could get my hands on," recalls Hamlett. "And of course I credited my sources in the plan."

Once you've measured the market and the demand for your product, you need to define strategies for marketing and pricing. The marketing plan of action spells out the best ways to reach potential customers — direct marketing, advertising, and special promotions are all possibilities. As for prices, you'll need to say how you plan to set them, based on standard markup, costs, perceived value, etc.

3. Financials

Having spent years critiquing and collecting business plans, Joseph Mancuso is quick to proclaim that well-considered financial calculations are the make-or-break element of any plan. Says he: "Anyone who's going to put in real money will look here first."

But don't stiffen at the mention of pro forma balance sheets and cash-flow forecasts. There is plenty of help to guide you along. Mancuso recommends the standardized, step-by-step "Projection of Financial Statements" forms available from Robert Morris Associates in Philadelphia. Other choices include workbooks from the Small Business Administration and computer programs for writing business plans.

Unless you're a veteran numbers cruncher, the tools mentioned above will serve only as a guide. To make sure your tabulations are realistic, work closely with a recognized accountant. "A potential lender or investor can compare your numbers to similar businesses," reminds Thomas. "If your figures are way out of line, they'll be skeptical of what you have to say."

The basic components of the financial section are as follows:

Balance sheets list a company's assets and liabilities. You'll need to construct two of these tools — an "opening day" balance sheet, which is a current financial snapshot of your business; and a "projected balance sheet," which shows how these figures are likely to change over time. The balance sheets should be updated yearly.

The *statement of income* compares your total revenues against all expenses, such as salaries, office supplies, insurance, marketing costs, etc. Organized by fiscal year, these tables are used to determine net income and should be updated every 12 months to show your company's progress.

Cash-flow forecasts chart the movement of funds in and out of your business. These numbers give you an idea of how much money you will need to fulfill your business' mission. They can also alert you to periods when you'll be short on cash. Depending on the purpose of the plan, the experts recommend you forecast three to five years out, and bankers consider any loan over one year as long-term. "Most investors want out within five to seven years," says Mancuso. "You ought to have a plan that shows them getting out and how much money they'll be taking with them."

One calculation they'll want to see — and that you should include in this section — is a "break-even analysis." Basically, this type of forecast tells a potential investor how much time you'll have to carry the business before it makes a profit. To figure it out, calculate the business' fixed and variable costs, then measure them against projected revenue. "Break-even" is when revenues match costs.

Even if you're not seeking outside dollars just yet, the financial section of your plan — especially the cash-flow forecast — is useful for predicting how well your company might perform over time. Los Angeleno Chris Floyd found out the hard way. He hawked fax paper from his garage for two years before taking a free course on business-plan writing at the University of Southern California. It sold him on the power of numbers. "Our business was already doing well by the time I went to USC," recalls Floyd. "But by following the numbers in the plan, we saw almost immediately that we could take the business further." His company, Images Business Systems, is today a major distributor of Xerox machines and papers, and had sales of $2.3 million in 1990.

4. The Management Team

Impressive facts, figures and forecasts will fall flat without a knowledgeable team behind them. Round out your plan, then, with biographies of yourself and other managers in the company. "Investors want to know as much as possible about the decision-makers of a company," says Howard University's Flake. Treat these bios as expanded resumes, spelling out each person's role and financial stake in the company. Also include a detailed history of all companies you or your associates have run in the past, emphasizing any specific roles that speak to the business at hand. Novices with no business background are best advised to state their inexperi-

ence — though they should note any relevant skills, degrees, certifications, or other credibility boosters. If you plan on bringing more than five players on board, you may want to include an organization chart that shows the precise hierarchy within your company. If you haven't done any hiring yet, flesh out this section by describing each management post and how you intend to fill it.

5. Tailor and Update Your Plan

Because business plans are goal-oriented documents, you may need to prepare several versions to accommodate multiple audiences. The basic format will remain the same, but text should change to address the inevitable questions from financiers, employees, or partners.

Ken Shead, president of the Drew Pearson Cos., constructed three separate plans of action for the Dallas-based **BLACK ENTERPRISE 100s** firm. New to the market, the sportswear manufacturer sought lucrative licensing agreements with the NBA, NFL, Disney World, and other brand-name organizations. The problem: Shead had to prove to each that he understood their market, their seasonality and image. "We had to do a separate market analysis for every license contract we went after," says Shead. "And once we landed the contracts, we had to take a snapshot of each one for

yet another plan to bring to the bank."

Understanding such needs will help you determine what should be amplified in the plan. Lenders, who want to be repaid, will zero in on your cash flow. Venture capitalists care about track records and crave detailed biographies, as they calculate their eventual payout.

"The basic formula for all plans is the same," says Clark of Xavier University. "But different industries will want to expand certain areas." Success in retailing, for instance, hinges on "location, location, location." So retailers should include a site analysis in their market overview. Construction firms, on the other hand, need to figure costs on a job-by-job basis — their financial calculations, then, will be more complex.

As your company changes, so should your plan. New employees may necessitate a longer management section; a cash infusion will require updates in your financials. Expanded product lines, new branches — all of these are reasons to update your plan. "I never expected any of this to be easy," says Floyd, who says he has revised his plan six times to keep up with his business. "Our plan is definitely a work in progress."

How to Write a Winning Plan

Define Your Product or Service. What exactly do you aim to sell? Once you've nailed down the mechanics of your product or service, concentrate equally on its strengths — or weaknesses — in relation to quality, price, and service. To make sure your concept is focused, bounce the idea off of several trusted colleagues and family members.

Research Your Idea. Aside from doing market research in your area, visit a similar city to check up on businesses like yours. You might also try an informal survey of potential customers. Construct graphs, tables, and charts to illustrate your findings and include in your plan.

Figure Your Start-Up Costs. Estimate both the start-up and future costs of running your business. Factor in at least three months' worth of raw

materials, office space, supplies, salaries, taxes, marketing, etc. Don't overlook legal and accounting fees. Such costs, reflected in your cash-flow forecast, help gauge how long you'll have to carry the business.

Says Xavier University professor Thomas Clark: "There are uncertainties you can't account for, but the point is to position yourself well enough to absorb the shock."

Read Several Plans Before Writing Yours. Before you sit down to write your own, take the time to review several other business plans — preferably in your field. Ask your colleagues, banker, or another potential audience member to show you their idea of a top plan. You may spot something you've missed.

Bolster Your Knowledge. Contact colleges or business organizations in

your area to find out about any plan-writing primers. Many, such as the five-day course taken by Los Angeles entrepreneur Chris Floyd, are free. Take advantage of free advice sessions offered by the Small Business Administration and the Centers for Minority Business Development.

Write Your Own Plan. Don't shrug off the chore of writing a business plan on a so-called "pro." While many sources can provide valuable advice, no one can speak for your business better than yourself. Hire a proofreader to review your plan.

Get the Tone Right. In polishing the plan, concentrate on your writing style. Strive for a confident tone, but spare the reader any self-congratulatory prose.

Source: November 1991 Black Enterprise *magazine, The Earl G. Graves Publishing Co., Inc., New York, NY 10011. All rights reserved.*

THE BUSINESS PLAN THAT GETS THE LOAN

By Louise Washer

It's 5:30 in the evening and Margi Showers shifts gears as she pulls onto highway 235. She's headed for the home of her former colleague and new business partner, Caren Christensen. The two meet almost every evening at this time. So far they have completely outlined the idea for their new retail business, and they've named the shop-to-be the Lagniappe, a Creole word for "little gift." Now comes the tough part: developing a business plan.

Caren has quit her job at a nonprofit company to devote herself full-time to the venture. Margi plans to resign as soon as she and Caren secure a loan and find a location.

Leaving her management job, Margi knows, will be difficult emotionally — she's taking a big risk. "I'm 47 years old and divorced. Should I really throw away the financial security of my job?" Margi asks herself as she cruises down the interstate. She has 20 more years to work. And she knows she needs to make good use of them to prepare for retirement.

The way Margi looks at it, now is a good time to take the risks involved in starting a business. If the venture doesn't fly, she still has plenty of time to establish herself somewhere new. If the shop does take off, it will take a good 10 years to grow it big. Their long-term plans include franchising.

They're still taking a huge risk, though, and Margi is nervous. That's one reason she's so determined to succeed. And the key to success, she knows, is planning. Writing their business plan will be one of the most important things Margi and Caren do for their business.

Caren also has a lot at stake. Both her family in Sioux Falls, South Dakota, and her husband are successful entrepreneurs. This is her chance to prove she can be one, too. "I always wanted to go into the family business," she tells Margi during one of their evening planning sessions. "I wanted to go to the gemological institute and then help run our jewelry business. My father really discouraged that. He wanted me to finish college. So I did. My brother is the one who went into the business."

Defining their Mission

By the time Margi turns off the highway and winds her way toward Caren's, she has overcome her ambivalence about becoming an entrepreneur. She's ready to take on any challenge, including writing a business plan.

To prepare for this task, she and Caren have ordered pamphlets, bought books and attended seminars. They've tapped information from the local Small Business Development Center (SBDC), the Iowa Development Corporation, and the Women's Economic Development Group Enterprises (WEDGE). They have notes on how to write a business plan: what to include, how to get their point across, where to find information, how to estimate sales.

Once at Caren's house, Margi heads for the kitchen, where they'll hold their meeting. She hoists a four-inch stack of these notes and other information onto the table.

"I've been thinking," Margi says as she and Caren sit down. "Writing a business plan is a lot like writing a grant application — and I've done loads of those." She pulls out a clean notebook and slips her sandals off to get more comfortable.

"First you come up with an idea and research it. Then you put everything down on paper," she says. "The more information you have that says this is not a risky proposition, the more chance you have of getting the grant. The same should go for doing our business plan and getting our loan."

"OK, sounds easy," Caren says sarcastically. "We make a great case for why our business will be a raving success, and the bank will just shower us with money. But how do we actually get started?" She glances at their stacks of information and groans.

"I think we should start with iced tea," says Margi. "And then I guess we should do what the books say: state our mission and, you know, the nature of the business."

Caren and Margi work our their mission statement: "...to build a retail business that meets the needs of those who are seeking originality in their personal and home accessories..." They go on to define the Creole word *lagniappe*: "a gift given a customer at the time of purchase." They explain that the store will sell local handicrafts as well as jewelry and home accessories.

Their notes tell them the next section in the business plan should discuss the target customer. Since identifying the customer was an integral part of coming up with the business concept, Margi and Caren already have done the research in this area. Now they have to put it all together in writing.

According to David Thornburgh, director of the Wharton Small Business Development Center, "The easiest way to identify your customer is to ask yourself to describe in detail the first shopper you picture walking into your store." If you do that, he says, it forces you to ask all the right questions, such as: How much education does she have? What's her household income? What are her tastes and preferences? Where does she live? What magazines does she read?

Thornburgh confirms that Caren and Margi are on the right track with their estimate that the ideal customer for their high-end crafts and accessories is a woman, 25 to 55 years old, in a two-income family earning more than $45,000 a year. Before this meeting, Caren and Margi had gone to the library and dug up a copy of the latest Des Moines census. They found that their target customer is in the top 11 percent income bracket and that she lives in one of five specific suburbs. They put all this information into the business plan.

With a rough draft of this section done, Caren and Margi call it quits. The next hurdle they face is one of the toughest: settling on a location and rounding out their research on the competition.

Location Is Everything

As Wharton's Thornburgh says, "In retail, no matter what you're selling, location is key. You've got to be where there are people with an interest in your product and with the money to buy it." Margi and Caren know who their target customer is; they just have to figure out where she shops. They stake out the top shopping malls, Ingersoll Avenue (a main shopping strip) and the Valley Junction (the newly renovated downtown of West Des Moines, one of the suburbs their target customer lives in).

They take notes on who shops where and check the library for shopper surveys. This digging turns up a poll of Valley Junction shoppers showing that their ages and incomes exactly fit those of the Lagniappe's target market.

Margi and Caren also take into account walk-by traffic as opposed to drive-by traffic. "One big advantage that the malls and the Valley Junction have is that people tend to walk up and down window-shopping," Caren remarks one afternoon while the two are scouting the Valley Junction.

"I know. If we have to count on people driving specifically to our shop, it could take forever to build sales. And unless the bank *gives* us our start-up funds, we won't have forever," adds Margi.

"I wish we had statistics on walk-by traffic," says Caren. "The advice we've gotten on how to write a convincing business plan always says to list supporting statistics..."

"What it doesn't tell is how to get those statistics," finishes Margi.

"Maybe we should just sit here and count the number of people who walk by," Caren suggests. Margi likes the idea, and the two choose the following Friday to stage their count. They watch six shops, counting the number of people who go in each.

They already were leaning toward the Valley Junction as their first-choice location. The results of the count make the decision easy. In their business plan, they report that between 11:30 AM and 12:30 PM, an average of 18.6 people enter each store. That number reaches 25 between 2:15 and 3:15. They project that 764 people visit each store from Monday through Friday. Business triples on weekends, according to store owners. Though competition for space in the Valley Junction is fierce, rates are relatively low at about $7 a square foot, compared with $25 or $30 at the malls.

Checking Out the Competition

During all this location scouting, Margi and Caren manage to kill two birds with one stone by seeing what potential competitors are up to. They'll need to discuss the competition in their business plan in order to explain the specific niche they plan to fill.

They comb Des Moines looking for any operation close to what theirs will be. They look at the way merchandise is being displayed and marketed. They casually ask questions: "How long have you been here?" Or, "Your logo seems so familiar. Do you do much advertising?"

"Most people don't do enough of this type of homework," says William Dunkelberg, PhD, dean of the School of Business and Management at Temple University in Philadelphia. "If others are doing something similar to what you plan to do, go watch them — even if they're in another town. There are enough surprises out there as it is. Take the opportunity to see what problems they encounter. Find out what kind of business you can reasonably expect to do."

For their next meeting a week later, Margi arrives at Caren's with a rough draft

of the section on competition. With the exception of one store two hours away in Iowa City, they have found no retailer that duplicates their idea. She lists many of the stores they've visited and explains that although quite a few carry manufactured jewelry and accessories, none mixes these products with crafts by local artisans. That's the niche Caren and Margi are after.

Together they add a new paragraph supporting the viability of that niche. They explain that their idea is similar to that of the very successful annual Des Moines festival Art in the Park. They quote a coordinator of the festival stating that demand is on the rise for crafts and jewelry created locally.

Promoting their Brainchild

In planning their promotional strategy, Margi again takes advantage of her background in grant-application writing. "I love this part," she tells Caren over the phone one evening after typing up some ideas. "What do you think of this as the slogan for our initial ad campaign: 'If you liked Art in the Park, you'll love the Lagniappe'?

"I've pinpointed six papers we should run ads in," she continues. "Now I need your help planning a party for before we open. I think we should have that *and* a grand opening — just to make a big splash."

Later, descriptions of these launch ideas go into the business plan, as does their idea for giving away lagniappes with each purchase. By the time Margi finishes listing her plans for promoting and advertising, the section fills five pages of the business plan.

Over the next few weeks, Margi and Caren add six smaller sections to their plan. They describe pricing strategies, staffing plans, customer services (such as guarantees), their buying plan, their inventory system, and what the store will look like. Now the partners are ready to move on to what will be their biggest challenge: the financials.

Getting to the Bottom Line

Margi and Caren know how important it is to get the numbers right in their business plan. These bottom-line figures will be crucial in convincing a potential lender that the Lagniappe is a good risk. With that in mind, Caren buys a copy of *Accounting for the Non-Accountant* and plans to attend two SBA-sponsored seminars on accounting, bookkeeping, and taxes.

In the meantime, the partners need to project their sales figures. "In other words, how many scarves, earrings, and sculptures we can reasonably expect to sell in our first year," Caren explains to

Margi on the steps of the Des Moines Public Library, where the two have met to do some research.

In search of industry statistics, they check the *Encyclopedia of Associations* for sources. From the Jewelers of America, Inc., they learn that jewelry stores average sales of $140 per square foot, with the top 2 percent at $381. Caren finds out that her family's jewelry business grosses $400 per square foot. For the business plan, Caren and Margi calculate that fine jewelry, 20 percent of their business in a 1,200-square-foot store, will produce about $62,400 in sales.

They do similar calculations for hand-crafted jewelry, personal accessories and home accessories. Estimated total sales for the first year come to $160,000.

Next they figure start-up costs: They list $10,350 for fixing up the space, buying display cases, and so on. Starting inventory adds $12,100. That number is low, since 60 percent of their inventory will be on consignment from artisans. Operating capital for the first year will be $20,000. Other expenses add $3,800, bringing the total to $46,250.

The financial projections in their business plan will list these costs as well as Caren and Margi's sources of start-up capital. The two partners will invest $15,250; they seek a loan of $31,000.

Doing the Numbers Again

With one list done, the next — monthly operating expenses — becomes a little easier. Here they include salaries, rent, insurance, legal and accounting fees, interest and depreciation, to name a few. The total comes to $6,655 per month, or almost $80,000 a year. They'll use these numbers to project their annual income (for the next five years) and cash flow — the crux of the financial section.

Accounting for the Non-Accountant offers a clear guide to compiling the rest of the figures they need now. They've also hired an accountant to review their numbers. Margi and Caren meet, calculators in hand, every evening at Caren's; they do the numbers and redo them, almost endlessly it seems.

To project monthly cash flow, Margi and Caren must estimate the sales they'll generate and the inventory purchases they'll make each month. This is something they need help with. Their business is a very seasonal one — experts have told them they'll bring in 50 to 80 percent of their income in the 2 months before Christmas. Margi and Caren know that cash-flow problems are a common tripwire for new businesses. They turn to their accountant and the Small Business

Development Center, which provides advice and produces a spreadsheet showing a 12-month cash-flow analysis.

The last major calculations they need to do are a balance sheet, listing their assets and liabilities, and a break-even analysis, which shows the level of sales they'll need to break even at a given scale of operation. Once those are done, they breathe a huge sigh of relief. Now there are just a few holes to fill, and then their plan will be finished.

They put in a section on their management experience, followed by their resumes and letters of reference. Next they add a three-page discussion of risk factors, including the impending renovation of the street through the Valley Junction — a potential threat to customer access. Finally, they cover their future plans: franchising and manufacturing select merchandise.

Wooing the Loan Officer

While they're putting these finishing touches on their masterpiece, they begin scouting the banks. "Let's ask around: Who gives a lot of SBA-backed loans? And who's giving a break to women?" suggests Margi.

"I'll call the SBDC," Caren volunteers. "Maybe our accountant knows someone too." After thorough research, the partners settle on West Bank.

They set up a 10 AM meeting and wear their "power suits," as Margi calls them. "OK...her name is Michele Gregory," Margi mutters as the two approach the bank's entrance. "Now, we can't look nervous. We're cool."

They meet Michele, give her a copy of their 71-page, spiral-bound plan and begin explaining their concept. Michele flips right to the financials and scans the numbers while she listens. Every few minutes, she interrupts with a question. "Do you know about the street-repair plans for the Valley Junction? That will hurt sales," she says.

As soon as Margi and Caren wind down their presentation, Michele says, "This looks good. It's well written, but you have problems with your figures. You'll need more money for advertising, and your sales figures seem too high." She asks for a week to study the plan more closely.

Margi and Caren aren't really disheartened. Overall the meeting went well. That one week, however, seems to last a year.

At their next meeting, Michele lists areas that need further explanation or reworking. So, back at Caren's kitchen table, the two pull out their calculators yet again. They also revisit WEDGE and the SBDC for help. The result: a plan they're sure is better. But is it good

enough? Michele hears more than ten business proposals a week, and she grants loans to fewer than half, she's told them.

On the way to their third meeting, Margi's palms are sweaty. "Why am I so nervous?" she asks. "I've spoken before groups of 2,000 — this is one person." Caren laughs.

They arrive and hand Michele an 8-page memorandum containing their changes, including a new projected-income statement and cash-flow analysis. Michele looks slowly through the material. It's dead quiet in her office. Margi and Caren wait, stealing tense glances at each other.

Finally she looks up. She smiles, slaps her desk and says, "Let's do it!" Margi and Caren are so stunned they hardly react at first. Once outside in the parking lot, though, they hug each other and laugh so hard that Margi cries. "We got it!" Caren keeps saying, "Thirty thousand dollars!"

The only hitch in their plans is that Michele made their SBA-guaranteed loan contingent on their finding a space on the main street in the Valley Junction. Michele insists that this will be tougher than they think. But the two decide they'll worry about that tomorrow. Tonight they'll celebrate.

What Makes a Loan Officer Say "Yes"

It can be difficult to look objectively at a business plan you've been toiling over and tinkering with for weeks. What you think is critical may be of only marginal interest to a prospective lender. To help you fine-tune your plan, here's advice from loan officers who lend to small businesses.

Show you can hit the ground running. You don't need to have worked as a French chef to open a restaurant, but that (or similar) experience does give you extra leverage when you go for a loan. Be sure to include your resume in your business plan. "If you don't have something notable to put in, say whom you would hire to supply the skills you lack," says Deborah Nilson of First Bank National Association, Minneapolis.

Cash flow: Present the Good, the Bad and the Likely. Outline what-if sce-

narios as well as detailed monthly cash-flow projections for the first year. "We want to see that there's room for error before we lend," says Nilson. "And if not, tell us how you intend to raise additional equity if you meet tough times."

Make sales projections that reflect real life. "If I see a plan for a vacuum-cleaner shop that projects enough sales to support a family of five in the first month, the rest of the plan looks suspect," says Pat Julien of United Bank of Michigan. "On a start-up, there are always lower sales at the outset," adds Nilson. "We'd expect projections to increase as the business gains momentum."

Consult the experts on numbers. Never make rough guesses when you're putting together financials. Dun & Bradstreet and Robert Morris Associates

publish industry averages. Talk to other local business people, and call suppliers to ask about prices and volume discounts.

Don't shoot too high or too low. If you think you're doing the bank a favor by asking for a very small loan, think again. "I don't want to see a scaled-down, bare-bones proposal," says Pamela Steece of the Merchant's Bank in Burlington, Vermont. "It must adequately suit the needs of the business. And that means enough working capital to cover at least six months of fixed expenses." On the flip side, it's also a mistake to ask for too much. "No bank is going to do 100 percent financing on a start-up. You've got to inject at least 25 percent of the initial capital," says Kathleen Romano Jackson of New Jersey's Garden State Bank.

— Laurel Touby

3

DEVELOPING A SIMPLE BUSINESS PLAN: CLASSROOM LEARNING EXERCISES

This chapter demonstrates the process of writing a business plan. To some extent, the process has been simplified. We will provide an overview of a business plan but will avoid extensive elaboration of the subject matter. Our intention is to focus attention on the framework of the plan and the necessary information for putting it together.

As you later formulate personal plans for real ventures, you will need to amplify or modify this document as required by the characteristics of the specific venture. In most cases, for example, you should project cash flow on a monthly basis. In the sample plan, cash flow is presented only by years. The additional material presented in Chapter 4 will help you decide how to expand your "real-world" plan and will also make you aware of additional resources for developing those plans.

AN EXAMPLE OF A SIMPLIFIED PLAN

In this section of the chapter, we present a scenario for a potential small business and a simple business plan developed on the basis of that scenario. In a subsequent section of this chapter, other assignment scenarios are described as a basis for you to gain "hands-on" experience in developing a plan. By examining the completed plan for the first scenario, you should learn how to develop a plan for the assignment scenario(s). A set of worksheets is provided to assist you in this assignment.

The sample plan that follows will give you clues concerning what you need to cover when you develop your plan, but it will not provide all of the details. Since the business described in your plan will differ from the venture contemplated in this sample plan, you will need to develop sales estimates, cost figures, marketing approaches, and so on that are appropriate for that venture.

The Sample Plan Scenario (Report-Plus)

Valerie Wright is a sophomore English major attending Southern University, a small liberal arts college in southern Florida. She is the current president of the college journalism club which is where she first met her dorm roommate, Cheri Perez. Cheri is a junior computer science major. Valerie and Cheri have become good friends and have been discussing the possibility of a new business venture. Both entrepreneurs were born and raised in rural areas and feel a need to supplement the meager financial support currently provided by their parents.

After months of brainstorming, they have agreed to start a venture called "Report-Plus" which would serve the needs of students and local businesses for typing and binding reports and term papers. Both young entrepreneurs recently attended a seminar entitled "How to Start a New Business." From this experience, they realize the need for a basic business plan document to help them better visualize their business venture and also to assist in obtaining some additional financial resources.

THE SAMPLE PLAN
FOR REPORT-PLUS

▮ Executive Summary

Report-Plus is a startup business with two principals. Valerie Wright is a sophomore journalism major and Cheri Perez is a junior computer science major at Southern University in Emmett, Florida .

The new business will offer word-processing and related report preparation services to the students of Southern University and to local small businesses. The principals believe there is an opportunity to provide customers with a quality service which is not currently available.

There appears to be an unfilled demand for quality report preparation services on the university campus. Initial research has demonstrated a need for such services. Market projections estimate a potential business of 19,200 reports from Southern University students each 12-month period. Additionally, there are over 100 small businesses within two miles of the university which have indicated an interest in our service.

This business plan has been developed to provide a blueprint for operation and to introduce Report-Plus to prospective investors with the intention of borrowing $3,000 from a bank with an interest rate of 9 percent and obtaining another $3,000 from an equity investor to begin the operation of this business. The bank loan would need to be a 12-month note with the option of renewal each year, provided that everything is on track. The equity investor would need to invest another $1,000 at the end of the first year of operations.

▮ General Company Description

▪ *Name and Location*

Report-Plus is a startup business with two principals who will be involved in its development. The principal contacts are: Valerie Wright, Box 204, Emmett, Florida and Cheri Perez, 1302 North James Street, Emmett, Florida. The business will be located on the Southern University campus.

▪ *Nature and Primary Product or Service of the Business*

During the past 12 months, the principals have studied the need for a manuscript preparation service that would serve the needs of the Southern University campus and surrounding businesses. The mission of the company will be to take the rough draft materials of clients and transform them into reports of professional quality. We expect to completely satisfy our customers by maintaining a dedication to quality.

■ Current Status

This business venture will be started at the beginning of the next semester, assuming adequate funding is available. The primary efforts during the first semester will be directed to the student market and expanded as quickly as possible to the local business market.

■ Legal Form of Organization

The new business will begin operation as a partnership between Valerie Wright and Cheri Perez. Both partners agree to the development of a formal partnership agreement based on 50-50 division of workload and profits once the business venture is funded.

Products and/or Services

■ Description of Products and/or Services

The main service of our firm will be the preparation of term papers for students and business reports for business clients. In addition to the word-processing service, we will also provide a graphics service. Some bindery services will also be available to create a professional-quality report for customers. Report-Plus will also carry a limited line of related products such as pens, paper clips, Liquid Paper, and other such products. Sales from these products and services should be about $2,000 per year.

■ Superior Features or Advantages Relative to Competing Products or Services

All of these reports will be created using the most advanced computer hardware and word-processing programs available. We will also print reports by using the latest high-quality laser printers. This service will be a substitute for handwritten reports and reports typed by students and office personnel in small businesses.

■ Any Available Legal Protection — Patents, Copyrights, Trademarks

There is no legal protection available for our service, but we will feature the business name Report-Plus so that loyalty can be developed on the basis of quality work.

■ Dangers of Technical or Style Obsolescence

The increasing use of computers by individual students and small businesses will make preparation of reports easier for students and for small businesses. However, most do not currently have adequate equipment, expertise, or desire to perform this work. Over the long run, of course, the per-capita demand for the service may decrease.

▮ Marketing Plan

▮ *Analysis of Target Market and Profile of Target Customer*

The primary target market for our services will be the 12,000 students of Southern University. We estimate that the majority of the students are enrolled in classes each semester which require 2-3 reports ranging from 5 to 50 pages in length. The secondary target market consists of businesses in the local city of Emmett, Florida which has an SMA population of approximately 150,000. There is an office building complex and two strip malls within two miles of the university, containing more than 100 separate small businesses.

There is no competition for our business located directly on the Southern University campus with the exception of a few duplicating machines and coin-operated typewriters in the university library.

Most students are currently writing their papers using the business school computer lab, which is always crowded. The lab has 15-20 computers which are linked to only one printer that is frequently not working. Those students who go off-campus for word-processing services appear to respond to advertisements on campus billboards or in the local newspaper.

Most small businesses located in the local business district are using their own equipment for word-processing and one or two local print shops for quality printing and binding service.

▮ *How Customers Will Be Identified and Attracted*

Since most students prepare reports or papers of some type, practically all students can be recognized as potential customers. The students who write more reports are those at the junior and senior level and those in graduate school. Businesses with fewer than 50 employees are also potential customers because of limitations on their internal resources for such work.

Customers will be attracted by advertising and a limited amount of personal selling.

▮ *Selling Approach, Type of Sales Force, and Distribution Channels*

The service will be sold directly to student users and to business firms. Based on advertising and/or conversations with satisfied customers, we anticipate that customers will bring their materials to us.

We expect to make some sales calls, as time permits, on small business firms in the area. We will take samples of our work to use in such sales presentations.

■ *Types of Sales Promotion and Advertising*

The advertising projected for this service is as follows:
1. Student newspaper advertising
2. Direct mail to dormitory students and selected small businesses
3. Bulletin board notices

■ *Credit and Pricing Policies*

Most sales will be made on a cash basis. However, credit for 30 days will be available to business customers. Pricing structure will be as follows:

$ .90   per original page
  .06   per page for additional copies
1.00   for binding

■ Management Plan

■ *Management-Team Members and their Qualifications*

Valerie Wright
    Sophomore English major at Southern University
    High school valedictorian
    GPA to date: 3.75
    GPA in all English courses: 4.0
    Good typing skills

Cheri Perez
    Junior computer science major at Southern University
    GPA to date: 3.4
    GPA in all computer courses: 4.0
    Work experience: two semesters as assistant in
      university computer laboratory
    Good typing skills

■ *Other Investors and/or Directors and their Qualifications*

Professor Henry Cunningham, who teaches marketing and entrepreneurship courses at Southern, has counseled with us regarding our new venture plans. He is willing to talk with us informally from time to time about our progress and developments in the business.

■ *Outside Resource People and their Qualifications*

Our business will be too small initially to require the services of a CPA. We will need an attorney to help prepare the partnership agreement, and we plan to consult with Professor Carolyn Gilbreath, J.D., for this purpose.

■ *Plans for Recruiting and Training Employees*

Initially, we plan to perform all of the work ourselves. As the volume grows and as we need temporary help during peak periods, we expect to recruit well-qualified fellow students. We would expect to select only those with knowledge and expertise validated by classroom performance. Training requirements should be minimal.

Operating Plan

Operating or Manufacturing Methods Used to Produce the Product or Service

Work assignments will normally be processed in the order in which they are received. Reports will be typed on a computer, using Microsoft Word, and printed on a laser printer.

Description of Operating Facilities (Location, Space, Equipment)

We have an option for a rent-free office in the university student activities building. This arrangement was negotiated based on the understanding that we will provide the university with a special pricing schedule after 12 months of operation. Our facility is 20 feet by 30 feet and has all necessary lighting, electrical outlets, and furniture.

Our initial operation will include two personal computers with word-processing, spreadsheet, and database programs. One laser printer and one duplicating machine will also be needed. The cost of the equipment will be $17,000.

The equipment will be depreciated on a straight-line basis over a five-year life. The vendor for the computer equipment will loan the firm $10,000 against the purchase price of the equipment. The loan's principal is to be repaid at the rate of $2,000 per year plus interest on the remaining balance of the loan each year.

Quality-Control Methods To Be Used

The computer system for checking spelling of words will be used. Also, the material will be scanned by the operator after entry. Materials will be spot-checked by carefully reading pages from one or more finished reports each day to identify any basic flaws in the system.

Procedures Used to Control Inventory and Operations

Work projects will be assigned a control number as received, and a log listing all projects will be maintained. Completion will be noted on the log, and completed reports awaiting pickup will be stored in cabinets or on shelves according to customer name.

Sources of Supply and Purchasing Procedures

Principal supply items (particularly paper) will be purchased from local dealers such as Office Depot and Chesser's Office Supply. Every effort will be made to control costs by competitive price shopping.

Financial Plan

Revenue and Expense Projections for Three Years

We have made the following projection of revenues and expenses:

	Year 1	Year 2	Year 3
Campus market reports	19,200	19,200	19,200
Campus market share	3%	5%	7%
Estimated reports serviced	576	960	1,344
Total business market reports	1,000	1,000	1,000
Business market share	6%	10%	12%
Estimated reports serviced	60	100	120
Expected revenues from miscellaneous supplies	$2,000	$3,000	$5,000
Cost of labor per report	$12.00	$12.00	$12.00
Cost of material per report	$0.50	$0.50	$0.50
Selling expenses as a percentage of total dollar sales	8%	8%	8%
Projected owners' salaries	$6,000	$8,000	$10,000

Other assumptions include:
- The average report length will be 16 pages for students and 30 pages for businesses, producing an average $20 in revenues per student report and $40 per business report.
- On average, students will want one copy of their report in addition to the original; businesses will want five copies. We will charge six cents per page for additional copies.
- Practically all copies of reports will be bound for a charge of $1 each.
- The effective income tax rate will be 20 percent.
- In addition to the equipment needs stated earlier, we will be extending credit for Report-Plus's business customers. The accounts receivables should be about 15 percent of annual sales. Also, inventories should run about 12 percent of annual sales. However, our suppliers should provide credit to us, which we have estimated at 10 percent of annual sales.

Sales projections related to the preparation of student term papers and reports are based on the following assumptions:
- Eighty percent of the 12,000 students at the university, or 9,600, prepare at least two reports each 12-month period. This gives a projection of 19,200 (9,600 x 2 = 19,200) reports.
- Report-Plus will obtain 3 percent of the student business in the first year, increasing to 5 percent and 7 percent in the following two years, respectively.

Revenue forecasts associated with the businesses needing Report-Plus services are based on the following assumptions:

■ On average, the 100 local businesses will need at least 10 reports each 12-month period.

■ Report-Plus will obtain 6 percent of the business market in the first year, increasing to 10 percent and 12 percent in the following two years, respectively.

The financial results of the assumptions being made are presented in the accompanying appendix which includes a pro forma income statement, balance sheets, cash flow statements, and financial ratios.

APPENDIX

Report-Plus
Pro forma Financial Statements

■ *Pro forma Income Statement*

	Year 1	Year 2	Year 3
Sales			
Campus	$11,520	$19,200	$26,880
Business	2,400	4,000	4,800
Total sales — reports	$13,920	$23,200	$31,680
Duplicating services	1,093	1,822	2,370
Binding	876	1,460	1,944
Miscellaneous supplies	2,000	3,000	5,000
Total sales	$17,889	$29,482	$40,994
Cost of goods sold			
Labor	$ 7,632	$12,720	$17,568
Materials	318	530	732
Total cost of goods sold	$ 7,950	$13,250	$18,300
Gross Income	$ 9,939	$16,232	$22,694
Operating expenses			
Depreciation	$ 3,400	$ 3,400	$ 3,400
Selling expenses	1,518	2,359	3,280
Owners' salaries	6,000	8,000	10,000
Total operating expenses	$10,918	$13,759	$16,680
Operating income	($ 979)	$ 2,473	$ 6,014
Interest expenses	1,270	1,070	870
Earnings before taxes	($ 2,249)	1,403	5,144
Taxes	0	0	860
Net income	($ 2,249)	$ 1,403	$ 4,284

■ *Pro forma Balance Sheet*

	Beginning	Year 1	Year 2	Year 3
Assets				
Cash	$ 2,000	$ 2,434	$ 4,765	$10,099
Accounts receivable	0	360	600	720
Inventories	1,000	2,147	3,538	4,919
Total current assets	$ 3,000	$ 4,941	$ 8,903	$15,738
Gross fixed assets	17,000	17,000	17,000	17,000
Accumulated depreciation	0	(3,400)	(6,800)	(10,200)
Net fixed assets	$17,000	$13,600	$10,200	$ 6,800
Total assets	$20,000	$18,541	$19,103	$22,538
Liabilities and Net Worth				
Accounts payable	$0	$ 1,789	$ 2,948	$ 4,099
Bank loan	3,000	3,000	3,000	3,000
Total current liabilities	$ 3,000	$ 4,789	$ 5,948	$ 7,099
Equipment loan	10,000	8,000	6,000	4,000
Total liabilities	$13,000	$12,789	$11,948	$11,099
Equity				
Partners' contribution				
Valerie Wright	$ 2,000	$ 2,000	$ 2,000	$ 2,000
Cheri Perez	2,000	2,000	2,000	2,000
Other investor(s)	3,000	4,000	4,000	4,000
Total partners' contributions	$ 7,000	$ 8,000	$ 8,000	$ 8,000
Accumulated profits (losses)		(2,249)	(846)	3,439
Total partners' equity	7,000	5,751	7,154	11,439
Total liabilities and equity	$20,000	$18,541	$19,102	$22,538

■ *Pro forma Cash Flow Statement*

	Year 1	Year 2	Year 3
Operations			
Net income	$(2,249)	$ 1,403	$ 4,285
Add:			
Depreciation	3,400	3,400	3,400
Increases in accounts payable	1,789	1,159	1,151
Deduct:			
Increases in accounts receivable	360	240	120
Increases in inventories	1,147	1,391	1,381
Total cash flows from operations	$ 1,433	$ 4,331	$ 7,335
Investing	$0	$0	$0
Financing			
Equipment loan (payments)	($2,000)	($2,000)	($2,000)
Other investor	1,000	0	0
Total cash flows from financing	($1,000)	($2,000)	($2,000)
Total cash flows	$ 433	$ 2,331	$ 5,335

■ *Financial Ratios*

		Year 1	Year 2	Year 3
Current ratio	current assets / current liabilities	1.03	1.50	2.22
Quick ratio	current assets - inventories / current liabilities	0.58	0.90	1.52
Operating income ROI	operating income / total assets	−5.3%	13.0%	26.7%
Operating profit margin	operating income / sales	−5.5%	8.4%	14.7%
Asset turnover	sales / total assets	0.96	1.54	1.82
Debt/total assets	total liabilities / total assets	69.0%	62.6%	49.3%
Return on equity	net income / total partners' equity	−39.1%	19.6%	37.5%

BUSINESS PLAN
ASSIGNMENT SCENARIOS

Having shown the simplified sample plan, we now present some alternative scenarios to permit you to gain experience in preparing such a plan.

■ (A)

Plan a business to sell blankets or clocks specially designed with school logo to alumni of your school. Develop this idea to include each of the sections developed in the sample plan for the Report-Plus plan. Use the following blank worksheets for your work.

■ (B)

Plan a business to sell corsages prior to a homecoming or other special athletic event at your school. Develop this idea to include each of the sections developed in the sample plan for the Report-Plus plan. Use the following blank worksheets for your work.

■ (C)

Plan a business to sell advertising space on calendars or directories of some type to be distributed free to students. Develop this idea to include each of the sections developed in the sample plan for the Report-Plus plan. Use the following blank worksheets for your work.

■ (D)

Conceptualize an original business venture which you believe has merit. Develop this idea to include each of the sections developed in the sample plan for the Report-Plus plan. Use the following blank worksheets for your work.

WORKSHEET A

■ Executive Summary

_____
_____
_____
_____
_____
_____
_____
_____
_____
_____
_____
_____
_____
_____
_____
_____
_____
_____
_____
_____
_____
_____
_____
_____
_____
_____
_____
_____
_____
_____
_____
_____
_____
_____
_____

WORKSHEET B

■ General Company Description

Name and Location

_____
_____
_____
_____
_____
_____
_____
_____
_____

Nature and Primary Product or Service of the Business

_____
_____
_____
_____
_____
_____
_____
_____
_____
_____
_____
_____
_____
_____
_____
_____

WORKSHEET B *(cont.)*

Current Status

_____
_____
_____
_____
_____
_____
_____
_____
_____
_____
_____
_____
_____

Legal Form of Organization

_____
_____
_____
_____
_____
_____
_____
_____
_____
_____
_____
_____
_____
_____
_____
_____
_____
_____
_____
_____
_____

WORKSHEET C

■ Products and/or Services

Description of Products and/or Services

_____

_____

_____

_____

_____

_____

_____

_____

_____

_____

Superior Features or Advantages Relative to Competing Products or Services

_____

_____

_____

_____

_____

_____

_____

_____

_____

_____

_____

_____

_____

_____

_____

_____

_____

_____

WORKSHEET C *(cont.)*

Any Available Legal Protection — Patents, Copyrights, Trademarks

_____

_____

_____

_____

_____

_____

_____

_____

_____

_____

_____

_____

Dangers of Technical or Style Obsolescence

_____

_____

_____

_____

_____

_____

_____

_____

_____

_____

_____

_____

_____

_____

_____

_____

WORKSHEET D

■ Marketing Plan

Analysis of Target Market and Profile of Target Customer

_____
_____
_____
_____
_____
_____
_____
_____
_____
_____
_____

How Customers Will Be Identified and Attracted

_____
_____
_____
_____
_____
_____
_____
_____
_____
_____
_____
_____
_____
_____
_____
_____
_____

WORKSHEET D *(cont.)*

Selling Approach, Type of Sales Force, and Distribution Channels

_____

_____

_____

_____

_____

_____

_____

_____

_____

Types of Sales Promotion and Advertising

_____

_____

_____

_____

_____

_____

_____

_____

_____

_____

Credit and Pricing Policies

_____

_____

_____

_____

_____

_____

_____

_____

_____

_____

_____

WORKSHEET E

■ Management Plan

Management-Team Members and their Qualifications

_____
_____
_____
_____
_____
_____
_____
_____
_____
_____
_____

Other Investors and/or Directors and their Qualifications

_____
_____
_____
_____
_____
_____
_____
_____
_____
_____
_____
_____
_____
_____
_____
_____
_____
_____
_____

WORKSHEET E *(cont.)*

Outside Resource People and their Qualifications

_____

_____

_____

_____

_____

_____

_____

_____

_____

_____

_____

_____

Plans for Recruiting and Training Employees

_____

_____

_____

_____

_____

_____

_____

_____

_____

_____

_____

_____

_____

_____

_____

_____

WORKSHEET F

■ Operating Plan

Operating or Manufacturing Methods Used to Produce the Product or Service

_____
_____
_____
_____
_____
_____
_____
_____
_____

Description of Operating Facilities (Location, Space, Equipment)

_____
_____
_____
_____
_____
_____
_____
_____
_____
_____

Quality-Control Methods To Be Used

_____
_____
_____
_____
_____
_____
_____
_____
_____

WORKSHEET F *(cont.)*

Procedures Used to Control Inventory and Operations

_____

_____

_____

_____

_____

_____

_____

_____

_____

_____

_____

_____

Sources of Supply and Purchasing Procedures

_____

_____

_____

_____

_____

_____

_____

_____

_____

_____

_____

_____

_____

_____

_____

_____

_____

WORKSHEET G

■ Financial Plan

Revenue and Expense Projections for Three Years

_____
_____
_____
_____
_____
_____
_____
_____
_____
_____
_____
_____
_____
_____
_____
_____
_____
_____

Needed Financial Resources

_____
_____
_____
_____
_____
_____
_____
_____
_____
_____

WORKSHEET G *(cont.)*

Sources of Financing

_____

_____

_____

_____

_____

_____

_____

_____

_____

_____

_____

_____

_____

_____

_____

_____

_____

_____

_____

_____

_____

_____

_____

_____

_____

_____

_____

_____

_____

_____

_____

_____

_____

_____

4

PREPARING A COMPREHENSIVE BUSINESS PLAN

I n this chapter, we offer guidance for preparing a complete business plan. First, we briefly consider some suggestions for writing the plan, thoughts about the format, and what we can do to make the presentation more effective. Then we look at some of the content matters in designing the plan. Next, we recommend selected references and computer software programs for preparing a business plan. Finally, we provide examples of two business plans:

- A business plan prepared by a student group in a field studies course
- An actual plan developed by an individual interested in starting a firm

Any sample plan should be viewed as an attempt by an individual or group to present an analysis of a proposed venture. No plan is perfect, and this is especially true for plans prepared by students. While the sample plans will not correspond exactly to yours, they will help you see what is involved in preparing a complete plan.

FORMAT AND WRITING
SUGGESTIONS

The quality of a completed business plan depends on the quality of the underlying business concept. A defective venture idea cannot be rescued by good writing. A good venture concept may be destroyed, however, by writing that fails to communicate.

The business plan must be clearly written and relatively short — typically under 40 pages. Use the plan to give credibility to your ideas. When you make a claim, such as a promise to provide superior service or an assessment of the attractiveness of the market, offer strong supporting evidence for your position. Above all, make sure the plan is believable.

Skills of written communication are necessary to present the business concept in an accurate, comprehensible, and enthusiastic way. Brevity does not permit discussion of general writing principles here. Nevertheless, it may be useful to include some practical suggestions specifically related to the business plan. Following are some hints given by the public accounting firm Arthur Anderson and Company in their booklet, *An Entrepreneur's Guide to Developing a Business Plan*:

1. Provide a table of contents and tab each section for easy reference.
2. Use a typewritten 8 1/2" x 11" format and photocopy the plan to minimize costs. Use a loose-leaf binder to package the plan and to facilitate future revisions.
3. To add interest and improve comprehension—especially by prospective investors who lack the day-to-

day familiarity that your management team has—use charts, graphs, diagrams, tabular summaries, and other visual aids.

4. You almost certainly will want prospective investors, as well as your management team, to treat your plan confidentially, so indicate on the cover and again on the title page of the plan that all information is proprietary and confidential. Number each copy of the plan and account for each outstanding copy by filing the recipient's memorandum of receipt.

5. Given the particularly sensitive nature of startup operations based on advanced technology, it is entirely possible that many entrepreneurs will be reluctant to divulge certain information—details of a technological design, for example, or highly sensitive specifics of marketing strategy—even to a prospective investor. In that situation, you can still put together a highly effective document to support your funding proposal by presenting appropriate extracts from your internal business plan.

6. As you complete major sections of the plan, ask carefully chosen third parties—entrepreneurs who have themselves raised capital successfully, accountants, lawyers, and others—to give their perspectives on the quality, clarity, reasonableness, and thoroughness of the plan. After you pull the entire plan together, ask these independent reviewers for final comments before you reproduce and distribute the plan.

CONTENT OF THE BUSINESS PLAN

A prospective entrepreneur needs a guide to follow in preparing a business plan. Although there is no one standard format in general use, there are many similarities among the general frameworks proposed for business plans. A simple condensation or overview of the major segments common to many of these organizing patterns was provided in Figure 2 in Chapter 1. The suggested sections of the plan were given as follows:

- Executive Summary
- General Company Description
- Products and Services Plan
- Marketing Plan
- Management Plan
- Operating Plan
- Financial Plan
- Legal Plan[1]
- Appendix of supplementary materials

With the overview of the above elements of the business plan identified, let's consider each part of the plan, along with some of the important questions that must be answered. A business plan for each new venture is unique. Therefore, we are unable to cover every question to be

---

[1] In contrast to the original list shown in Figure 3 in Chapter 1, we have separated the legal plan from the company description, as frequently is done in complete business plans.

addressed. However, we can address some of the questions common to many business plans.

■ Executive Summary

This section is crucial in getting the attention of the five-minute reader. It must, therefore, convey a clear picture of the proposed venture and, at the same time, create a sense of excitement regarding its prospects. This means that it must be written and rewritten to achieve clarity and interest. Even though it comes at the beginning of the business plan, it summarizes the total plan and must be written last.

■ General Company Description

The body of the business plan begins with a brief description of the company itself. If the firm is already in existence, its history is included. By examining this section, the reader will know, for example, whether the company is engaged in retailing or construction or some other line of business, where the business is located, and whether it is serving a local or international market. In many cases, issues noted in the legal plan—especially the form of organization—are incorporated into this section of the plan. Some important questions to be addressed in this section of the plan include:

1. Is this a startup, buyout, or expansion?
2. Has this business started operation?
3. What is the firm's mission statement?
4. When and where was this business started?
5. What is the basic nature and activity of the business?
6. What is its primary product or service?
7. What customers are served?
8. Is this company in manufacturing, retailing, service, or another type of industry?
9. What is the current and projected state of this industry?
10. What is the company's stage of development — "seed stage," full product line, or what?
11. What are its objectives?
12. Does the company intend to become a publicly traded company or an acquisition candidate?
13. What is the history of this company?
14. What achievements have been made to date?
15. What changes have been made in structure or ownership?
16. What is the firm's distinctive competence?

■ Products and Services Plan

As implied by the title, this section discusses the products and/or services to be offered to customers. If a new or unique physical product is involved and a working model or prototype is available, a photograph should be included. Investors will naturally show the greatest interest in products that have been developed, tested, and found to be functional. Any innovative features should be identified and patent protection, if any, explained. In many instances, of course, the product or service may be similar to that offered by competitors—for example, starting an electrical contracting firm. However, any special features should be clearly identified. Important questions to be answered in this section of the plan include:

1. What product or service is being offered?
2. What does the product look like?
3. What is the stage of product development?
4. What are the unique characteristics of the product or service?
5. What are its special advantages?
6. What additional products or services are contemplated?
7. What legal protection applies—patents, copyrights, or trademarks?
8. What government regulatory approval is needed?
9. How does the product relate to the state of the art for such products?
10. What are the dangers of obsolescence?
11. What dangers are related to style or fashion change?
12. What liabilities may be involved?
13. How has the product been tested or evaluated?
14. How does the product or service compare with products or services of competitors?
15. What makes this firm's service superior?

■ Marketing Plan

As stated earlier, prospective investors and lenders attach a high priority to market considerations. A product may be well engineered but unwanted by customers. The business plan, therefore, must identify user benefits and the type of market that exists. Depending upon the type of product or service, you may be able not only to identify but also to quantify the user's financial benefit — for example, by showing how quickly a user can recover the cost of a product through savings in operating cost. Of course, benefits may also take the form of convenience, time saving, greater attractiveness, better health, and so on.

The business plan should follow the establishment of user benefits by documenting the existence of customer interest, and showing that a market exists and that customers are ready to buy the product or service. The market analysis must be carried to the point that a reasonable estimate of demand can be achieved. Estimates of demand must be analytically sound and based on more than assumptions if they are to be accepted as credible by prospective investors. The marketing plan must also examine the competition and present elements of the proposed marketing strategy—for example, by specifying the type of sales force and methods of promotion and advertising that will be used. Key questions to be answered in this section of the plan include:

Market Analysis

1. What is your target market?
2. What is the size of your target market?
3. What market segments exist?
4. What is the profile of your target customer?
5. How will customers benefit by using your product or service?
6. What share of the market do you expect to get?
7. What are the market trends and market potential?
8. What are the reactions of prospective customers?
9. How will your location benefit your customers?

Competition

1. Who are your strongest competitors?
2. Are their businesses growing or declining?
3. How does your business compare with that of competitors?
4. On what basis will you compete?
5. What is the future outlook of your competitors?

Marketing Strategy

1. How will you attract customers?
2. How will you identify prospective customers?
3. What type of selling effort will you use?
4. What channels of distribution will you use?
5. In what geographic areas will you sell?
6. Will you export to other countries?
7. What type of sales force will you employ?
8. What special selling skills will be required?
9. What selling procedures will be used?
10. How will you compensate your sales force?
11. What type of sales promotion and advertising will you use?
12. What pricing policy will you follow?
13. What credit and collection policy will you follow?
14. What warranties and guarantees will you offer?
15. How do your marketing policies compare with those of competitors?
16. How will you handle seasonal peaks in the business environment?

■ Management Plan

Prospective investors look for well-managed companies. Unfortunately, the ability to conceive an idea for a new venture is no guarantee of managerial ability. The plan, therefore, must detail the organizational arrangements and the backgrounds of those who will fill key positions in the proposed firm.

Ideally, investors desire to see a well-balanced management team — one that includes financial and marketing expertise as well as production experience and inventive talent. Managerial experience in related enterprises and in other startup situations is particularly valuable in the eyes of outsiders reading the business plan. Some critical questions to be answered in this section of the plan include:

1. Who are members of the management team?
2. What are the skills, education, and experience of each?
3. What other active investors or directors are involved, and what are their qualifications?
4. What vacant positions exist, and what are the plans to fill them?
5. What consultants will be used, and what are their qualifications?
6. What is the compensation package of each key person?
7. How is the ownership distributed?
8. How will employees be selected and rewarded?
9. What style of management will be used?
10. How will personnel be motivated?
11. How will creativity be encouraged?
12. How will commitment and loyalty be developed?
13. How will new employees be trained?
14. Who is responsible for job descriptions and employee evaluations?
15. What time frame has been developed to accomplish the company's objectives?

■ Operating Plan

This section of the plan shows how you will produce the product or provide the service. It touches on such items as location and facilities—how much space you will need and what type of equipment you will require. The importance of the operating plan varies from venture to venture, but this plan is necessary even for firms providing services. The operating plan should explain the proposed approach to assuring production quality, controlling inventory, using subcontracting, or meeting other special problems related to raw materials. Some important questions to be answered in this section of the plan include:

1. How will you produce your product or service?
2. What production will be accomplished by subcontracting?
3. What production or operating facilities will be used?
4. What is the capacity of these facilities?
5. How can capacity be expanded?
6. What methods of production will be used?
7. What type of plant layout will be used?
8. What production control procedures will be used?

9. What quality control system will be used?
10. How will inventory be controlled?
11. What is the environmental impact of the business?
12. What are the advantages and disadvantages of the location?
13. What production or operating advantages exist?
14. What are the labor requirements?
15. What are the major production costs?
16. What materials or components are critical to production?
17. What sources of supply exist?
18. What will be the production cost at each level of operation?

Financial Plan

The financial analysis constitutes another crucial section of the business plan. In it, the entrepreneur presents projections of the company's financial statements, or pro forma statements, over the next five years or even longer. The forecasts include balance sheets, income statements, cash flow statements, and break-even analysis. These pro formas, as they are called, should be prepared on a monthly basis for the first year, quarterly for the second and third years, and annually for the remaining years. It is vitally important that the financial projections be supported by well-substantiated assumptions and explanations on how the projections and costs are determined.

While all the financial statements are important, we should give special attention to understanding the cash flows, because a business may be profitable, but fail miserably at producing positive cash flows. Through the cash flow statement, we will see the sources of cash—how much will be raised from investors and how much will be generated from operations. It also shows how much money will be devoted to such investments as inventories and equipment.

Within this section, the plan should indicate clearly how much cash is needed by the prospective investors, and the intended purpose for the money. Lastly, the investor needs to be told how and when he or she may expect to cash out of the investment. Most investors want to invest in a privately-held company for only a finite time period. They want to know what mechanism will be available for their exiting the company. Experience tells them that the eventual return on their investment will be largely dependent on their ability to cash out of the investment. Important questions to be answered in this section of the plan include:

1. What assumptions are used for financial projections?
2. What revenue level is projected by months and years?
3. What expenses are projected by months and years?
4. What profits are projected by months and years?
5. What cash flow is projected by months and years?
6. What financial position exists now, and what is anticipated at various points during the next five years?

7. When will the business break even?
8. What financial resources are required now?
9. What additional funds will be required?
10. How will these funds be used?
11. How much has been invested and loaned by the principals?
12. What additional potential sources will be explored?
13. What proportions of funding will be debt and equity?
14. What type of financial participation is being offered?

■ Legal Plan

In the legal plan, the entrepreneur sets out the form of organization. The three major alternatives are proprietorship, partnership, and corporation. There are variations, however, that deserve consideration. A special type of corporation, for example, may serve to minimize federal taxes paid by the firm and its owners. As noted earlier, the legal plan does not necessarily stand as a totally separate section of the business plan but is often made a part of the general company description. The legal issues are important, however, and deserve careful consideration. Important questions to be answered in this section include:

1. Will the business function as a proprietorship?
2. Will the business function as a general or limited partnership?
3. Will the business function as a regular corporation or Subchapter S corporation?
4. What are the legal liability implications of the form of organization chosen?
5. What are the tax advantages and disadvantages of this form of organization?
6. Where is the corporation chartered?
7. What was the date of incorporation?
8. What attorney or legal firm has been selected to represent the firm?
9. What type of relationship exists with this attorney or law firm?
10. What legal issues are presently or potentially significant?
11. What licenses/permits may be required?
12. What insurance will be taken out on the business, the employees, and so forth?

■ Appendix

The appendix should contain various supporting materials and attachments that are not primary issues but complement the reader's understanding of the plan. These would include items of interest that were referenced in the text of the business plan. Examples would include: resumes of the key investors and managers; photographs of products, facilities, and buildings; professional references; market research studies; pertinent published research; signed contracts of sales; and other such materials.

WHERE TO GO FOR MORE INFORMATION ABOUT BUSINESS PLANS

The above presentation of the business plan offers a relatively in-depth survey of the business plan. More complete descriptions are provided in entire books on the subject and computer software designed to guide you through the preparation of the business plan. A listing of some of these references and a description of three such software packages are given in the next section. There are a host of others.

■ References on Preparing Business Plans

A partial list of references that could be helpful in preparing a real-world business plan include the following:

Abrams, Rhonda M. *The Successful Business Plan: Secrets and Strategies,* 2nd ed. Grants Pass, Oreg.: Oasis Press, 1993. $21.95.

Bangs, David H., Jr. *The Business Planning Guide: Creating a Plan for Success in Your Own Business,* 6th ed. Dover, N.H.: Upstart Publishing, 1992. $19.95.

Business Plan for Small Service Firms. U.S. Small Business Administration. No cost.

Luther, William M. *The Start-up Business Plan.* New York City: Prentice Hall, 1991. $14.

McKeever, Mike. *How to Write a Business Plan,* 4th ed. Berkeley, Calif.: Nolo Press, 1992. $19.95.

Pinson, Linda, and Jerry Jinnett. *Anatomy of a Business Plan,* 2nd ed. Chicago: Enterprise/Dearborn, 1993. $17.95.

Pinson, Linda and Jerry Jinnett. *Business Plan for the Small Construction Firm.* U.S. Small Business Administration, 1990. No cost.

Pinson, Linda and Jerry Jinnett. *Business Plan for the Small Retailer.* U.S. Small Business Administration, 1990. No cost.

Rich, Stanley R., and David E. Gumpert. *Business Plans that Win $$$: Lessons from the MIT Enterprise Forum.* New York City: HarperCollins, 1987. $12.

Schilt, W. Keith. *The Entrepreneur's Guide to Preparing a Winning Business Plan and Raising Venture Capital.* Englewood Cliffs, N.J.: Prentice Hall, 1990. $28.95.

Writing an Effective Business Plan, Deloitte & Touche.

■ Business Plan Software

There are many business plan computer software packages. However, the same basic objective exists for all these plans — to help you think through the important issues in beginning a new company and to organize your thoughts into an effective presentation.

Drawing from this wide variety of offerings, we have selected three software packages to profile. These are:

Inc. Business Plan, developed by *Inc.* Magazine

How to Write a Business Plan, prepared by the American Institute of Small Business

Business Disc Entrepreneur's Kit, offered by Maryland Institute Technologies

These software packages are described in the following sections.

■ *Inc. Business Plan*

The *Inc.* plan software provides a first-time user with the tools needed to get through with relative ease, which may or may not be in the best interest of the preparer — it is only with careful thought that a quality plan will result.

To start the program, the user is taken through a series of instructions set up to show how the program works and how to access different parts of the plan. The instructions are brief and to the point.

Once the user is into the program, getting started with actual data is quite simple. Each step is explained and described in terms of the information needed. By pressing the F1 key, a screen will appear to give help and advice in answering questions or moving to the next section.

The plan is organized along conventional lines. The detail of the plan is comprehensive in each section, including such small details as insurance and workers' compensation.

Level of detail:	Very comprehensive
Cost:	$139.00
Address:	INC Business Resources
	350 N. Pennsylvania Ave.
	P.O. Box 1365
	Wilkes-Barre, PA 18703-1365
	(717) 822-8899

■ *How to Write a Business Plan*

The setup of this software takes the user through the plan with ease. The basic idea with this software is to help the user build a business plan by using already written text, giving 5-6 different options in each section. In so doing, the text explains the basic points contained in a business plan.

The software is designed to be used with WordPerfect and Lotus 1-2-3, but it will run with Word for Windows and Excel. However, some of the calculations in the financial part of the plan have to be done outside the spreadsheet.

The organizational plan of the software includes such areas as the executive summary, general company description, a description of the firm's products or services, industry conditions, a marketing plan, production plan, and a financial plan.

Level of detail:	Moderate
Cost:	$125.00
Address	American Institute of Small Business
	7515 Wayzata Blvd.
	Minneapolis, MN 55426
	(612) 545-7001

■ *Business Disc Entrepreneur's Kit*

The Business Disc Entrepreneur's Kit primarily targets small business start-ups. Its main purpose is to assist a new company to develop a very simple but efficient business plan in the area of operations.

The Kit consists of two separate programs: the Business Disc and the Data/Companion program, which can be used together or separately. However, using both packages provides a wider range of possible modifications to the plan. The program is more or less an expert system because of the built-in questions which the user has to address to go through the development process.

The program is a DOS-based application, which could be run on a stand-alone computer or a network environment. It can be used in conjunction with a video disc. The program can be installed on a hard drive in about ten minutes.

The program begins with a brief tutorial on how to use the keyboard, especially the function keys. Specific roles played by these keys are highlighted. This makes it a bit easier for less experienced computer users to feel comfortable prior to development of a business plan.

The program contains four main modules: the business profile, personal income statement, cash flow projections, and the letter of intent. In each of the modules, the user has to make a series of decisions. Depending on the business area chosen, the program generates the appropriate questions to assist the user in considering important questions. All the information is saved on a data/companion diskette, which can be used separately with Lotus 1-2-3 once the model is built. Also, with an additional utility program called FisCal, a sensitivity analysis can be performed to show the effect of changes in certain key variables in the model.

Level of detail:	Moderate
Cost:	$29.95 [student version]
Address:	MITEC
	P.O. Box 1054
	456 Main Street
	Reisterstown, MD 21136
	1-800-526-0526

SAMPLE BUSINESS

PLANS

■ *Whitewater Golf Business Plan* —
a plan developed by a student group as a class
assignment, p. 57.

■ *Product Development & Marketing Co.* —
an actual plan developed for a start-up venture,
p. 81.

B U S I N E S S   P L A N   F O R

Whitewater Golf

Source: Used by permission of Morry Cole, Jennifer Barry, Chris Parr and Chris Mahlen.

■ Whitewater Golf Business Plan

TABLE OF CONTENTS

Plan Submitted By: Morry Cole: Group Leader, Financial Advisor   Chris Parr: Marketing Strategy
    Jennifer Barry: Products & Services   Chris Mahlen: Operations Plan
    Jennie Lannin: Market Research   Doug Dover: Legal Plan, Incorporation

WHITEWATER GOLF

Waco's Famlly Funplex

Morry Cole, Group Leader
Jennifer Barry
Doug Dover
Jennie Lannin
Chris Mahlen
Chris Parr

Executive Summary

The Company

Whitewater Golf is a startup business venture researched and developed by a four-man, two-woman entrepreneurship team. The team leader and principal contact is Morry Cole, 1909 South Ninth Street, Waco, Texas 76706 (817-753-4013).

This group came together with the idea of providing a fun, clean atmosphere of family entertainment for the people of Waco/McLennan County in Texas. This idea takes the form of a miniature golf complex that includes a miniature golf course, batting cages, an arcade, a family/party room, and a snack bar.

Whitewater Golf is confident of its market potential. The company plans on providing a safe, happy family atmosphere that will keep up with the community's needs and wants. With little existing rivalry in the area, Whitewater Golf intends to fill the opening left by its competitors.

Based on financial calculations made by the management team, Whitewater Golf calls for an initial investment of $290,000 to commence company operations. This investment will provide for the building of the complex and the supplying of equipment needed plus provide for beginning working capital.

Market Potential

Whitewater Golf is in a very positive market position. First of all, there is a significant lack of competition in the miniature golf area in Waco/McLennan County. The competition that exists is neglected and rundown and not in contention with the modern facilities that Whitewater Golf proposes. Also, Whitewater Golf market research shows that the amusement and recreation industry has increased its profits even during the economic recession.

Whitewater Golf plans to saturate the market via advertisements on television, in newspapers, on billboards, and in fliers. This will enable Whitewater Golf to reach the Waco/McLennan County population so that people will gain interest in the establishment and come enjoy our facilities.

The specific target audience Whitewater Golf would like to reach is a family: parents with children. Whitewater Golf would also like to reach teenagers, college students, and senior citizens.

Major Milestones

Whitewater Golf has managed to negotiate a promotional deal with Spalding where they will provide bats, batting helmets, putters, and golf clubs, as long as we only promote the Spalding name.

Distinctive Competence

Whitewater Golf has a distinct advantage over its competition. Whitewater Golf will provide a modern and safe place for families to come and take pleasure in. The company will also provide many facilities inside the complex besides just miniature golf for the entire family to enjoy. The competition is rundown and does not provide the safe environment nor the many facilities of Whitewater Golf.

Also, the well-roundedness of the fields of experience of the Whitewater Golf's founders helps considerably in the management and maintenance of the company. Morry Cole is a Finance major, Chris Mahlen is a Human Resource Management major, Chris Parr is a Marketing major, Jennifer Barry is a Business Administration major, Jennie Lannin is a Telecommunications major and Doug Dover is a Biology major.

Together this group has researched their proposal to build Whitewater Golf in the Waco/McLennan County area. They feel that this business entry will provide needed family entertainment and will show a positive profit.

■ Whitewater Golf Business Plan

Financial Summary

Based on the detailed financial projections by Whitewater Golf, if the company receives the required $140,000 in funding, it will operate profitably in year one. The following is a summary of the first year's projections.

YEAR ONE SALES: $168,824
YEAR ONE EXPENSES: $72,781

NET INCOME BEFORE TAX: **$91,553**
RETURN ON EQUITY: 61%

Industry

The Amusement Industry has experienced a 5-10% growth rate over the last few years which has been particularly noticeable in the amusement park sector. This industry is fortunate that it has continued to expand even throughout the recent recession. Affordable amusements and recreational facilities have maintained a steady demand in times of economic hardship.

According to the 1991 Amusement Industry Abstract, the miniature golf segment of the industry has experienced an increased emphasis in the past few years due to a trend towards smaller and more participatory amusements. Approximately 120,000,000 games of miniature golf were played in 1991 which is three times as many as an earlier estimate. The total demand for miniature golf is continuing to increase, while the number of new course openings is decreasing. While 32% of the courses were opened in 1990, only 5% were opened in 1991. This is inviting to potential entrants to the industry as the game's popularity is on the rise and the number of emerging companies is on the decline.

Year Built — Miniature Golf Courses

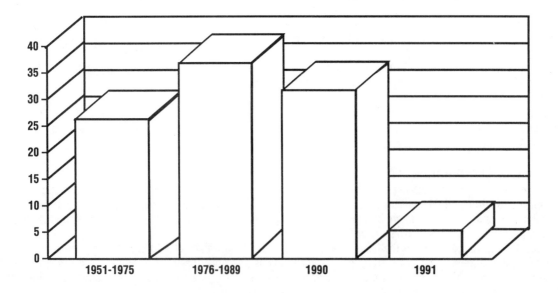

While the industry remains stable throughout economic fluctuations, it is much more sensitive to seasonal fluctuations. IAAPA's 1989 national Amusement Consumer Survey has concluded that miniature golf attendance clusters predominately into three summer months, particularly June, July, and August. Due to the moderate weather in Waco, Texas in the months of March, April, May, September, October, and November, the peak season in Waco has possibilities of extending much further than three summer months.

According to our survey, there is a strong need for more family-oriented recreational facilities in the Waco area. On average, consumers are willing to spend 5-10 dollars per visit and are planning to visit the facility twice a month and possibly once a week in the summer months. We are confident that the Waco area will be satisfied with the clientele that miniature golf attracts. According to the IAAPA, only 11% of the attendance nationwide is from the lowest household income category and 29% of the attendance comes from the highest income category.

Miniature Golf Attendance — 1989

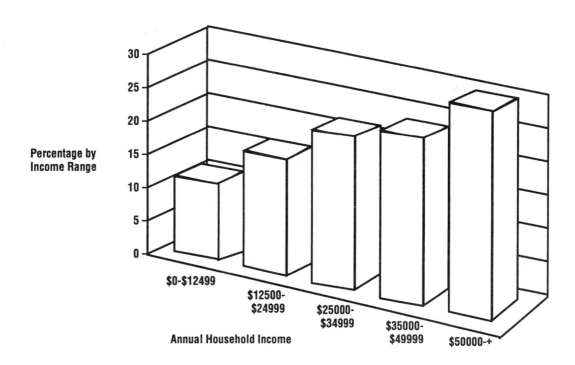

Percentage by Income Range

Annual Household Income

$0-$12499

$12500-$24999

$25000-$34999

$35000-$49999

$50000-+

— 3 —

■ Whitewater Golf Business Plan

The Company

Waco is in great need of an entertainment facility geared toward the family. In a city of nearly 200,000 people, there is only one miniature golf course. Due to a failure to update and innovate the course and facilities, the course has not been very successful. We are developing our facility as a family entertainment center. Not only are we going to offer an innovative golf course, but we will also offer batting cages, video games, and a snack bar. In order to accommodate clientele on their birthdays and other special occasions, we will maintain a party room that may be reserved for private parties. On the average, 59% of courses offer snack bars, 44% offer batting cages, and 41% offer bumper boats.

The contribution to revenue of each planned product and service is as follows:

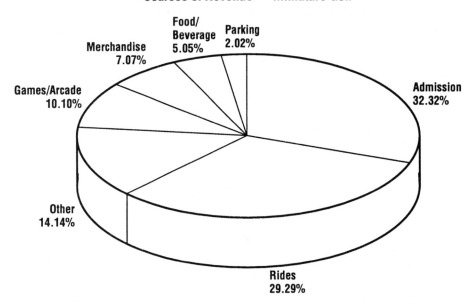

Sources of Revenue — Miniature Golf

- Food/Beverage 5.05%
- Parking 2.02%
- Merchandise 7.07%
- Games/Arcade 10.10%
- Admission 32.32%
- Other 14.14%
- Rides 29.29%

We intend to market the arcade and batting cages to a large extent to pull in significant revenues in addition to the golf fees. The bumper boat option is one we will bypass due to its large capital investment requirement. By using an innovative product design and product mix, this facility will meet and exceed the demands of Waco families and friends.

Entry and Growth

We will be entering the amusement/recreational market at full speed with the intention of obtaining a large market share within the first few months of business. Our short-run strategic plans are to employ extensive marketing geared towards the area families and church and school organizations. Promotions and special events at the facility will attract publicity and help to keep our marketing costs at a minimum.

Products and Services

Miniature Golf

Our company will offer three different golf courses and we will be leaving land for expansion in the future. Each hole will have a unique theme to it. Many of them will represent the sights and landmarks in Waco, Texas. Currently we are exploring the possibility of replicating the Alico building, Pat Neff, a Baylor Bear, and others. In addition, more challenging holes with swinging pendulums and other obstacles will also be offered. We are contracting with Alexander Brothers Lawns and Landscaping to do our landscaping that will be fairly extensive throughout the courses.

Batting Cages
Batting cages will be available for the many baseball and softball players in the area. Major league and slow pitch cages will be available. We will maintain three cages to begin with once again leaving room for later expansion. Bats and helmets will be available at a special booth near the cages.

Arcade
We will offer 15-20 video games inside the building. Variations include pinball, skeet ball, video golf, and others. Skeet ball will award tickets for certain high scores. A certain amount of tickets may be later turned in for a free game of golf. Video golf will allow avid golf players to participate in a golf game that involves teeing off and hitting the ball into a video screen. The video golf simulates the game for the player. The remaining games will be picked after future meetings with the video vendor. We will operate under a 50/50 split with the vendor. This involves no initial cost or installation fee. The profits will be split with the vendor and the vendor will cover all repairs. Our only cost is the electricity.

Snack Bar
Our snack bar will offer products that are particularly appealing to families. Our Blue Bell Bar will offer ice cream and soft drinks while the grill will serve hamburgers, hot dogs, french fries, and soft pretzels. Also, we will offer birthday cakes and party favors for private parties that utilize the party room.

Party Room
The party room will be available to anyone but will require an advanced reservation. It will be able to accommodate up to 50 people comfortably. It is adjacent to the snack bar and has a back door that leads out to the golf courses.

Customers

We are hoping to attract as many of all types of customers as we can: children, teenagers, college students, adults, and senior citizens. However, we plan to cater to the family enjoying a day or evening of entertainment together. This family, basically, is of a middle or upper-class income, a middle-aged, two-parent family with children. Parents tend to spend much more money when they go out with their children than when they go out alone, and we know that they will continue to do that when they visit our establishment. Even if only one parent takes the children out, we still expect to be able to take in the same amount of money, if not more.

Market Size and Trends

According to a Snapshot Market Report from the John F. Baugh Center of Entrepreneurship, there are approximately 189,000 people in the Waco/McLennan County area spending approximately $111 per person per year on amusement and recreation services. We want to capitalize on that monetary expenditure, so we plan to make Whitewater Golf something different to the area of Waco. Since there really is not a very competitive market for that type of entertainment here, we think that our place of business will be able to attract everyone from children to adults and senior citizens, teenagers to college students. We did a random phone survey of 74 people in the Waco/McLennan County area and found that most of them would go to a miniature golf course like the one we have proposed if it were opened.

■ Whitewater Golf Business Plan

Competition

Our only real competition is Lions Park. Lions Park is located on the corner of New Road and Bosque in front of Waco High School and looks like what you might find in an inner city slum. Lions Park has a Coke machine in case you are thirsty, but no snack bar, although RD's Hamburgers is right outside the miniature golf park. They do not have separate rooms for children's birthday parties or small, private parties. Park benches are the only places to sit, and their restrooms are similar to what you might find when you stop at a highway rest area. They also offer tennis courts, a swimming pool, and a kiddie land with about two rides and a kiddie slide, but they are all run-down and uncared-for. In addition, the entire park is encircled by tiny train tracks that one can only assume are used as a kiddie ride. Safety does not appear to be a major concern of theirs. They have no batting cages but Lions Park patrons could access Pat Zachary's Batting Cages located just across the street.

Our establishment will be a clean place with a relaxed atmosphere for people to come and enjoy themselves at a convenient location by Ryan's Steakhouse at the corner of Valley Mills Drive and Franklin Avenue. That alone would be enough to persuade customers to come to us instead of visiting Lions Park, but we also propose having a snack bar within our establishment with places to sit comfortably, a separate room for private parties, a game room, and batting cages in addition to our superior putt-putt courses on our lot. Moreover, our miniature golf park will not be just holes to put a ball into. We plan on designing each hole around our theme of "Whitewater," with extensive landscaping and waterfalls.

Estimated Market Share and Sales

In the beginning, we feel we will dominate the market over Lions Park, seizing seventy percent of the business market share in our first month. But as people see and hear our different media advertisements, hear positive word of mouth, and get familiar with our name and place of business, more and more patrons will come to us. Our goal is to eventually do a ninety-ten business market share over Lions Park and ultimately edge them out of business.

Ongoing Evaluation

At this particular time with the recession of our economy, we understand people are a little reluctant to spend money on anything except the necessities, but, in speaking with others in the same business, we found that their profits have only increased over time. Furthermore, we realize that trends and fads do not last for very long periods of time, so we plan to keep our place of business up to date with the community's demands in this area so that our customers will keep coming.

We are certain that our competition, Lions Park, will upgrade to meet the challenge we pose. However, with our modern facilities and our goal of staying current to the changing focus of the amusement industry, we feel that they cannot retake their market share.

Advertising

Advertising is a key element to any business. Advertising sparks people's interest, gives knowledge of a product, and creates a desire to use the product. Advertising is also a reminder of how, when, and where the consumer can use the product. Consumers need to be reminded that the product is out there and available for their use. In McLennan

County our product will be superior to any of our competitors and with our prime location we know no other golf business can compete.

Whitewater Golf will run three commercials a day on television. The first commercial will be in the afternoon while kids are watching their programs after school. This will stimulate an interest in the children and they will convince their parents to take them to Whitewater Golf. Two more commercials will run during prime time about two hours apart. This will cater to the adults watching sitcoms or movies. These commercials will run every other day for one week. The following week only two commercials will run every other day — again in the afternoon and sometime between 8:00 pm and 10:00 pm. These commercials will announce the grand opening of Whitewater and the times and location of the business. These television commercials will generate about 65% of the customers to our grand opening. Television commercials are proven to be the best source of advertising available to the public. This is why Whitewater Golf is putting so much effort into television advertising.

Another source of advertising is the newspaper. Whitewater Golf has decided to place an ad in *The Lariat*, Baylor University's campus newspaper. This will inform the college students of our new opening, location, hours, and specials. The newspaper will allow us to stay in contact with the students and provide them with information of our upcoming events.

Whitewater Golf has decided to place four billboards around the Waco area. The billboard will read **WHITEWATER GOLF** — Waco's Family Funplex. The first will be placed north of Waco on Highway 35 around the Bellmead area. This billboard will advertise to the residents of Bellmead, Lacy Lakeview, and people traveling into Waco from Hillsboro or Dallas. The second will be placed further up Highway 35 near the Baylor University campus. The third will again be on Highway 35 south of Waco. This billboard will attract people traveling in from the Temple/Killeen area or from Austin. The fourth will be on Valley Mills near Floyd Casey Stadium. This sign will let people know that we are just around the corner on Valley Mills and Franklin. These signs will contribute a lot of business from people coming into the Waco area or people out looking for something to do on the weekend.

Whitewater Golf has decided to pass out fliers at the high schools, supermarkets, college campuses, churches, and places of employment announcing our grand opening. This is designed for the grand opening only and will allow us to reach the customers that might have missed the television commercials, newspapers, and billboards. This is a rather cheap means of advertising; however, it has proven to be very effective in the past.

Pricing

Pricing is very important to any business. People are in business for one reason—to make money. We want to have a pleasant atmosphere, quality items, and the latest technology available for our customers at a reasonable price.

Miniature Golf	$5.00/18 holes for Adults $4.00/18 holes for kids (7-16) Under 7 free
Video Games	$1.00 = 5 tokens $5.00 = 30 tokens $10.00 = 50 tokens $25.00 = 125 tokens
*Batting Cages	$1.00 = 1 token (25 pitches) $4.00 = 5 tokens (125 pitches)

*Group rates are available for batting cages.

Discounts for 1 hour or more on the batting cages are available for teams that might want to take batting practice or for parties, etc. Group rates are available for groups of 10 or more people playing miniature golf. A dollar discount will be allowed for each eighteen holes.

Whitewater Golf will have a fabulous party room adjoining our game room. The room will seat 50 people comfortably. This room is designed for church groups, birthday parties, youth groups, and campus groups from the nearby colleges. We offer special rates for groups of 25 or more and for all church-related functions. We offer different rates for groups under 25. The party room package for any group starts with 15 tokens for each person, one

■ Whitewater Golf Business Plan

round of 18 holes of miniature golf, and free soft drinks. We will mention our party room in our commercial to help stimulate interest for its use.

Group rates for video games will be available in our party room package. Whitewater Golf plans to have discount coupons, holiday discounts (similar themes to Six Flags — holiday in the park, fright night, etc.), and buy-one-get-one-free nights, which will be one night out of the week when customers can buy a game of miniature golf and their partners play free. This offer is not for video games or batting cages. Whitewater has many exciting things planned for customers in the future.

Operations Plan

Location

Our facility will be located near the intersection of Valley Mills Drive and Franklin Avenue. The property is accessed from Franklin and is visible from both Valley Mills and Franklin. The property is currently held by Jim Stewart Realtors and is on the market for $42,000 an acre. There are ten acres for sale in the area but we have chosen a 1.5 acre plot. Whitewater will need 1.5 acres to accommodate both the facility and parking lot. The final sale price of the 1.5 acre lot is $62,650. The land is zoned as light industrial, and is currently unimproved, but all major utilities are "T'd" off at the rear of the lot.

This location is ideal for several reasons. First, it is visible from Valley Mills, which is the main artery of Waco and McLennan county. Second, it is located in the middle of the high traffic areas. Third, the land is about halfway between the Woodway area and Baylor, our two prime target markets. Finally, the location selected is very easy to find and is adjacent to one of Waco's biggest intersections.

Facilities and Improvements

The amusement facility proposed will consist of three main attractions. First, there will be thirty-six holes of miniature golf; next, we will have batting cages; and finally, there will be a game room/snack bar.

The estimate to build thirty-six holes of miniature golf from Alexander Brothers Lawns & Landscaping is $70,000 dollars. This estimate includes all the concrete work and all the decorating of each hole. We have a promotional deal from Spalding Inc. to acquire free putters and golf balls if we agree to use Spalding Inc. products exclusively at our facility.

Whitewater Golf will construct three batting cages. According to the industry abstract the total cost of these cages will be $67,600. The price of the cages includes balls, and the bats and helmets will come with the promotional program from Spalding Inc. The cages are self-feeding and therefore do not require an employee to run the equipment.

Whitewater Golf will also have a clubhouse that has a game room and snack bar. This building needs to be approximately 2,000 square feet to accommodate our needs. The cost of the building is estimated at $25,000 according to the *Marshall & Swift Real Estate Pricing Guide*. The estimate for the parking lot from the same source is $11,000. *Marshall & Swift* also estimated the lighting for the facility to be $2,500. For the game room, vendors will provide video games and maintain them in exchange for 50% of the revenue from them. This is perfect for us, because it does not require an initial cash outlay and does not tie up any equity in the games. It also allows us to receive immediate profit without an extended break-even point. Financially speaking there is virtually no risk.

The snack bar will offer basic items, such as nachos, hot dogs, ice cream, candy, and soft drinks. The first month's cost will be the highest due to the purchase of equipment. The first month's cost is projected to be $750, and the normal monthly operating cost will be $340. We were able to locate used equipment at Thompson Electric. To purchase a rebuilt heat lamp and crock pot for the nachos and a hot dog cooker from Thompson Electric will cost $160. A freezer for the ice cream with a display window will cost $250, and Coca-Cola will provide a soft drink dispenser at no cost with our agreement to advertise for them.

We will also need to purchase a cash register. Whitewater only needs one because the customer can pay for tokens, food, and golf at a cashier adjacent to the snack bar. We were able to locate a used cash register in the Fort Worth Star Telegram for $315. This particular model will print out inventory levels and sales by division at the end of the day. This will help us keep a finger on the pulse of the company. An additional expense will be a P.A. system that costs $500. We are going to purchase this from an individual (Joel Pinson) who was formerly in the band Blue Saint Kick and wants to sell the unused system. Insurance is another cost to be considered. According to State Farm, our annual insurance cost will be $1,368. This will cover liability and the fixed structures.

Strategy

The main strategy of Whitewater Golf is customer satisfaction. As with any service-oriented company, we are completely dependent on the customer's perception of the quality of service he or she is receiving. We are challenging our employees and management team to both constantly attract and retain customers. It is imperative that we provide an atmosphere that is acceptable to both adults and children and make both enjoy our facility. From an operations standpoint, our strategy is to cycle as many people through our golf courses and batting cages on a daily basis as possible. In summary, the main goal of Whitewater Golf is to satisfy the customer.

Management Team

The key ingredient of a successful management team is balance, and Whitewater Golf's management team has balance. Our management team is made up of Morry Cole, Jennifer Barry, Jennie Lannin, Doug Dover, Chris Parr, and Chris Mahlen. The balance spoken of earlier is achieved through the diverse educational background of the team: Morry Cole, Finance; Jennifer Barry, Business Administration; Chris Mahlen, Human Resource Management; Doug Dover, Biology; Chris Parr, Marketing; and Jennie Lannin, Telecommunications.

The organization of the team is that each will share equally in both profit and initial investment. Each of us will also serve as the board of directors. Chris Parr will actually work as the manager of the facility and draw a base salary of $20,000. An additional assistant manager (a Baylor student) will be acquired as a management intern. The intern will be paid $334 a month. The rest of the employees will be part time. Part-time employees are ideal for us because they require little compensation in both wages and benefits. At $6 an hour, our part-time employees will cost $27,914 annually. We will have to pay approximately 10% of payroll in the form of expenses to the state and local government. This 10% will cover unemployment compensation and social security charges. Whitewater Golf will not need to offer a benefits package because we will only have one employee exempt from the Fair Labor Standards Act. Our part-time help will be under the overtime and holiday pay provisions of the act, which requires that they be compensated time and one-half for overtime hours; therefore, our part-time help will work less than forty hours a week.

Hours of Operation

June - August
Mon - Thurs	12:00 - 9:00
Fri - Sat	11:00 - 10:00
Sun	2:00 - 10:00

September - November 10
Mon - Thurs	2:00 - 9:00
Fri - Sat	11:00 - 10:00
Sun	2:00 - 10:00

November 11 - March
Mon - Thurs	4:00 - 9:00
Fri - Sat	2:00 - 10:00
Sun	2:00 - 10:00

April - May
Mon - Thurs	2:00 - 9:00
Fri - Sat	11:00 - 10:00
Sun	2:00 - 10:00

We will be an equal opportunity employer and try to hire a diverse pool of employees. For example, we plan to hire from several EEOC protected classes: women, minorities, and older (above age 50) employees. With this diversity we will achieve a well-balanced work force. To establish a trustworthy work force, we will need to be selective and smart with our recruiting decisions. Obviously, a large pool of potential employees will be students, from both area high schools and Baylor. The main disadvantage of hiring students is that often when left without supervision, students tend to do favors for their friends. With the small nature of our firm, we cannot absorb the generosity of our employees. This is not to say a student is a bad choice, but rather we need to be selective and attempt to find and hire honest workers. Another large source of potential employees comes from the recent trend of hiring retired people for part-time employment. A retired individual could also bring experience to the organization. Honesty should be less of an issue with a retired individual as well.

Legal Plan

After careful consideration of all pertinent tax laws and liability considerations, all of the initial investors have come to the decision to file Whitewater Golf as a subchapter S corporation. Legal consultation with Mrs. Deedra Crow, a representative of the firm of Wesley J. Filer and Associates, has assured us that we meet all of the eligibility requirements to file as a sub S corp. Mrs. Crow has also agreed to remain as our local counsel for our corporation and continuing operations. There will be six hundred shares of stock issued equally among the six initial investors (100/person). Each share of stock represents one vote. Consequently, the decision-making power as well as the sharing of all profits will be equally distributed. Mrs. Crow has assured us that she will be able to handle our incorporation in its entirety for $1,200. Any further legal services will be $85/hour.

Accounting

The accounting firm of Patillo, Brown & Hill has been retained to look after all of the accounting aspects of our corporation including annual audits and preparation of quarterly financial statements. We have retained their services based on their reputation and to insure that any future financing will be based upon solid records from the past.

Financial Plan

The financing of our venture will come from two sources. $150,000 of the original investment will be provided by the owners. The remainder of our financing will be provided by a 9% ten-year fully amortized loan for $140,000. We will make certain that our loan has no prepayment penalty because we intend to pay it off early and utilize retained earnings to finance ourselves on a short-term basis. Detailed analyses of our start-up costs and our first year's operation are presented.

Whitewater's cash flow for the first year is detailed in the cash flow statement found on page 11. Loan amortization is presented on this statement as well as a listing of the start-up costs in great detail.

Whitewater Golf's year one beginning and ending balance sheets are found on pages 12 and 13 to present a snapshot of the company's position at our inception, and our projection for the end of our first year.

Our projected income for year one is presented in a month-by-month fashion on the operating plan found on page 14. Our sales figures are conservative numbers based on industry averages found in the industry abstract. Allocations have been made for foul-weather days and seasonality. Whitewater Golf—Waco's Family Funplex will proudly turn a profit in year one.

Whitewater Golf Incorporated: Cash Flow for Year One 1993-1994

CASH FLOW 1993-94													
													TOTAL
	JUNE	JULY	AUG.	SEP.	OCT.	NOV.	DEC.	JAN.	FEB.	MAR.	APRIL	MAY	
CASH ON HAND	150000	40620	63143	85665	99091	106507	110612	109528	108443	112328	121293	134418	
CASH RECEIPTS													
Putt-Putt Sales	0	18600	18600	11160	8868	6200	2700	2700	6200	8680	11160	12400	107268
Batting Cage Sales	0	4650	4650	4650	1550	1550	620	620	1550	4650	4650	4650	33790
Snack Bar Sales	0	5022	5022	3012	2395	1675	800	800	1340	1340	3012	3348	27766
Loan	140000	0	0	0	0	0	0	0	0	0	0	0	0
TOTAL CASH RECEIPTS	140000	28272	28272	18822	12813	9425	4120	4120	9090	14670	18822	20398	
TOTAL CASH AVAILABLE	290000	68892	91415	104487	111904	115932	114732	113648	117533	126998	140115	154816	
CASH PAID OUT													
Salaries	2396	2396	2396	2348	2348	2278	2264	2264	2264	2264	2348	2348	27914
Payroll Expense	239	239	239	234	234	227	226	226	226	226	234	234	2784
Supplies	400	25	25	25	25	25	25	25	25	25	25	25	675
Repairs	130	130	130	130	130	130	130	130	130	130	130	130	1560
Landscaping	200	200	200	200	200	200	200	200	200	200	200	200	2400
Advertising	2500	400	400	100	100	100	100	100	100	500	400	300	5100
Telephone	120	30	30	30	30	30	30	30	30	30	30	30	450
Utilities	600	300	300	300	300	300	200	200	200	300	300	300	3600
Insurance	114	114	114	114	114	114	114	114	114	114	114	114	1368
Taxes	118	118	118	118	118	118	118	118	118	118	118	118	1416
Interest	1050	1044	1039	1033	1028	1022	1016	1011	1005	1000	994	988	12230
Misc.	25	25	25	25	25	25	25	25	25	25	25	25	300
Incorporation Fees	1200	0	0	0	0	0	0	0	0	0	0	0	1200
Loan Principal Payment	723	728	734	739	745	751	756	762	768	773	779	785	9043
SUBTOTAL	9815	5749	5750	5396	5397	5320	5204	5205	5205	5705	5697	5597	70040
CAPITAL PURCHASES													
Cash Register	315	0	0	0	0	0	0	0	0	0	0	0	315
Sound/PA System	500	0	0	0	0	0	0	0	0	0	0	0	500
Courses	70000	0	0	0	0	0	0	0	0	0	0	0	70000
Building	25000	0	0	0	0	0	0	0	0	0	0	0	25000
Lighting	2500	0	0	0	0	0	0	0	0	0	0	0	2500
Parking	11000	0	0	0	0	0	0	0	0	0	0	0	11000
Land	62650	0	0	0	0	0	0	0	0	0	0	0	62650
Batting Cages	67600	0	0	0	0	0	0	0	0	0	0	0	67600
TOTAL CASH PAID OUT	249380	5749	5750	5396	5397	5320	5204	5205	5205	5705	5697	5597	
CASH POSITION	40620	63143	85665	99091	106507	110612	109528	108443	112328	121293	134418	149219	
OPERATING DATA													
Sales Volume		28272	28272	18822	12813	9425	4120	4120	9090	14670	18822	20398	168824
A/R (End of Month)	0	0	0	0	0	0	0	0	0	0	0	0	
Bad Debt (E.O.M.)	0	0	0	0	0	0	0	0	0	0	0	0	
Inventory (E.O.M.)	0	0	0	0	0	0	0	0	0	0	0	0	
A/P (E.O.M.)	750	340	340	340	340	340	340	340	340	340	340	340	
Depreciation	982	982	982	982	982	982	982	982	982	982	982	982	11784

■ Whitewater Golf Business Plan

Whitewater Golf Incorporated: Balance Sheet Beginning Year One

CURRENT ASSETS		LIABILITIES	
Cash	46171	CURRENT LIABILITIES	
Petty Cash	500	Current Portion of Long Term Debt	9043
Accounts Receivable	0	Notes Payable	0
Note Receivable	0	Accounts Payable	0
Inventory	750	Accrued Liabilities	0
PREPAID EXPENSES		Other Current Liabilities	0
Insurance	114	TOTAL CURRENT LIABILITIES	9043
Advertising	2500		
Supplies	400	LONG TERM LIABILITIES	
TOTAL CURRENT ASSETS	50435	Long Term Debt	130957
		TOTAL LONG TERM LIABILITIES	130957
CAPITAL ASSETS			
Cash Register	315	TOTAL LIABILITIES	140000
Sound/PA System	500		
Golf Courses	70000	OWNERS EQUITY	
Building	25000	Morry Cole, Capital	25000
Lighting	2500	Jennifer Barry, Capital	25000
Parking	11000	Doug Dover, Capital	25000
Land	62650	Jennie Lannin, Capital	25000
Batting Cages	67600	Chris Mahlen, Capital	25000
Total Capital Assets	239565	Chris Parr, Capital	25000
		Retained Earnings	0
Total Assets	290000		
		TOTAL OWNERS EQUITY	150000
		TOTAL LIABILITIES AND OWNERS EQUITY	290000

Whitewater Golf Incorporated: Balance Sheet End of Year One

CURRENT ASSETS		LIABILITIES	
Cash	150294	CURRENT LIABILITIES	
Petty Cash	500	Current Portion of Long Term Debt	21273
Accounts Receivable	0	Notes Payable	0
Note Receivable	0	Accounts Payable	340
Inventory	750	Accrued Liabilities	0
PREPAID EXPENSES		Other Current Liabilities	0
Insurance	114	TOTAL CURRENT LIABILITIES	21613
Advertising	2500		
Supplies	400	LONG TERM LIABILITIES	
TOTAL CURRENT ASSETS	154558	Long Term Debt	130957
		TOTAL LONG TERM LIABILITIES	130957
CAPITAL ASSETS			
Cash Register	315	TOTAL LIABILITIES	152570
Sound/PA System	500		
Golf Courses	70000	OWNERS EQUITY	
Building	25000	Morry Cole, Capital	25000
Lighting	2500	Jennifer Barry, Capital	25000
Parking	11000	Doug Dover, Capital	25000
Land	62650	Jennie Lannin, Capital	25000
Batting Cages	67600	Chris Mahlen, Capital	25000
Total Capital Assets	239565	Chris Parr, Capital	25000
		Retained Earnings	91553
Total Assets	394123		
		TOTAL OWNERS EQUITY	241553
		TOTAL LIABILITIES AND OWNERS EQUITY	394123

■ Whitewater Golf Business Plan

Whitewater Golf Incorporated: Operating Plan Year One

	JUNE	JULY	AUG.	SEP.	OCT.	NOV.	DEC.	JAN.	FEB.	MAR.	APR.	MAY	TOTAL
REVENUE													
Putt-Putt Sales	0	18600	18600	11160	8868	6200	2700	2700	6200	8680	11160	12400	107268
Batting Cage Sales	0	4650	4650	4650	1550	1550	620	620	1550	4650	4650	4650	33790
Snack Bar Sales	0	5022	5022	3012	2395	1675	800	800	1340	1340	3012	3348	27766
TOTAL REVENUE	0	28272	28272	18822	12813	9425	4120	4120	9090	14670	18822	20398	168824
COST OF SALES													
Snack Bar	750	340	340	340	340	340	340	340	340	340	340	340	4490
GROSS PROFIT	-750	27932	27932	18482	12473	9085	3780	3780	8750	14330	18482	20058	164334
EXPENSES													
Salaries	2396	2396	2396	2348	2348	2278	2264	2264	2264	2264	2348	2348	27914
Payroll Expense	239	239	239	234	234	227	226	226	226	226	234	234	2784
Supplies	400	25	25	25	25	25	25	25	25	25	25	25	675
Repairs	130	130	130	130	130	130	130	130	130	130	130	130	1560
Landscaping	200	200	200	200	200	200	200	200	200	200	200	200	2400
Advertising	2500	400	400	100	100	100	100	100	100	500	400	300	5100
Telephone	150	30	30	30	30	30	30	30	30	30	30	30	450
Utilities	600	300	300	300	300	300	200	200	200	300	300	300	3600
Insurance	114	114	114	114	114	114	114	114	114	114	114	114	1368
Taxes	118	118	118	118	118	118	118	118	118	118	118	118	1416
Interest	1050	1044	1039	1033	1028	1022	1016	1011	1005	1000	994	988	12230
Misc.	25	25	25	25	25	25	25	25	25	25	25	25	300
Incorporation Fees	1200	0	0	0	0	0	0	0	0	0	0	0	1200
Depreciation	982	982	982	982	982	982	982	982	982	982	982	982	11784
TOTAL EXPENSES	10104	6003	5998	5639	5634	5551	5430	5425	5419	5914	5900	5794	72781
													NET PROFIT YEAR ONE
NET PROFIT	-10854	21929	21934	12843	6839	3534	-1650	-1645	3331	8416	12582	14264	91553

Whitewater Golf Incorporated: Break-even Analysis

EXPENSES

FIXED EXPENSES

Principal Payment	9043
Insurance	1368
Depreciation	11784
Landscaping	2400
Interest	12230
TOTAL FIXED EXPENSES	36825

VARIABLE EXPENSES

Repairs	1560
Advertising	5100
Payroll	2784
Inventory	4490
Utilities	3600
Telephone	450
Supplies	675
Salary	2396
TOTAL VARIABLE EXPENSES	21055

TOTAL EXPENSES	57880
SALES	168824
BREAK-EVEN SALES IN DOLLARS	94705
MARGIN OF SAFETY IN DOLLARS	74119

Appendix

**The Securities Registration Division
State Securities Board**

Articles of Incorporation

■ Whitewater Golf Business Plan

Form Promulgated by the Secretary of State
for Articles of Incorporation for a Business Corporation

Articles of Incorporation

Article One

The name of the corporation is ___WHITEWATER GOLF INC.___
(Must contain Company, Corporation, Incorporated or an abbreviation thereof.)

Article Two

The period of duration is perpetual.
(May be for a number of years or until a date certain.)

Article Three

The purpose for which the corporation is organized is the transaction of any and all lawful business for which corporations may be incorporated under the Texas Business Corporation Act. *(Specific purposes may be stated).*

Article Four

The aggregate number of shares which the corporation shall have authority to issue is six hundred(600) of the par value of _One_ Dollars ($1.00) each. *(Shares may be of no par value.)*

Article Five

The corporation will not commence business until it has received for the issuance of shares consideration of the value of One Thousand Dollars ($1,000.00) consisting of money, labor done or property actually received.

Article Six

The street address of its initial registered office is 1909 S. 9th Street, Waco, TX 76706 and the name of its initial registered agent at such address is Morry S. Cole .
(Use the street, building or rural route address of the registered office; a post office box number is not sufficient.)

Article Seven

The number of directors constituting the initial board of directors is ___6___, and the names and addresses of the person or persons who are to serve as directors until the first annual meeting of the shareholders or until their successors are elected and qualified are:

_____

_____

_____

Article Eight

The name(s) and address(es) of the incorporator(s) is(are):

_____   _____

_____   _____

_____   _____

(signed)

_____ Incorporator(s)

Guidelines for Preparation and Filing of the Articles of Incorporation

1. Corporate Name

a. The corporate name must include one of the following words or abbreviations: Company, Corporation, Incorporated, Co., Corp., or Inc. [TBCA, article 2.05A(1)]. Limited, Ltd., or Unlimited do not meet the statutory requirement of article 2.05.

b. A corporate name may not include any word or phrase that implies a purpose not included in the articles of incorporation [TBCA. article 2.05A(2)].

Examples:

(1) Words appearing in a name that might imply an unlawful purpose are "accounting," "auditing," or "auditors," which imply practice of accountancy in violation of TEX. REV. CIV. STAT. ANN. article 41a-1. The same applies to words or phrases that imply the practice of law, medicine, or the like.

(2) The word "insurance" must be accompanied by other words, such as agency or services, that remove the implication that the corporate purpose is to be an insurer.

(3) The words "Bail Bonds" or "Surety" imply an unlawful purpose; these corporations ordinarily are filed with the State Board of Insurance.

(4) The words "Bank," "Banking," and the like, may not be used in a context which implies the purpose to exercise the powers of a bank. The Department of Banking can advise you on the efficacy of using "bank" or a derivation thereof.

(5) The word "Trust" may not be used by a corporation filed under the Texas Business Corporation Act.

(6) Words like "Co-op," "Cooperative," and the like, may not be used because all cooperatives are formed under specific enabling statutes and are otherwise governed by the Non-Profit Corporation Act.

(7) It is a violation of the Texas Engineering Practice Act, TEX. REV. CIV. STAT. ANN. article 3271A, for a corporation to use the words "Engineer" or "Engineering" in its name, unless it is engaged in the practice of engineering and its engineering services are performed by or under the supervision of a registered engineer. If this requirement is ignored, the Texas State Board of Registration for Professional Engineers will compel the corporation to change its name shortly after articles of incorporation are filed.

(8) A corporation that uses the words "Architect" or "Architecture" in its corporate name should determine from the Texas Board of Architectural Examiners whether such use is in violation of the statutes or rules applicable to the licensing of architects.

■ Whitewater Golf Business Plan

c. A corporate name shall not contain the word "lottery" [TBCA, article 2.05 A(4)].

d. Federal law generally precludes the use of the words "olympic" or "olympiad" unless authorized by the United States Olympic Committee. Refer to the Amateur Sports Act (Public Law 95-606).

e. The TBCA, article 2.05A(3), provides that a corporate name cannot be the same as, or deceptively similar to, or similar to, that of an existing domestic corporation, foreign corporation authorized to transact business in Texas, a name reservation, or name registration. The Texas Revised Limited Partnership Act provides that corporate and limited partnership names cannot be the same, deceptively similar or similar. In addition, the Texas Limited Liability Company Act provides that the names of limited liability companies, corporations and limited partnerships cannot be the same, deceptively similar, or similar.

A corporate name may be similar if a letter consenting to use of a similar name is obtained from the entity deemed to have the similar name. The letter of consent should be an unrestricted authorization for use of the name, signed by a corporate officer, a limited liability company manager or member, or a general partner of a limited partnership, and sent to the secretary of state with the articles of incorporation.

Please note that a letter of consent is an option with similar names only. If a name is the same as or deceptively similar to that of an existing entity, the name will not be filed under any circumstances.

f. A name should contain only symbols that are found on a standard typewriter keyboard. Distinctions between upper and lower case letters are ignored; our corporate records carry names in all capital letters. Subscripts, as in chemical formulas (H_2O), or superscripts and other mathematical symbols cannot be entered in our records.

g. The secretary of state determines whether a proposed corporate name is available in accordance with the rules on name availability adopted and filed in accordance with the Administrative Procedure Act. A complete set of rules can be found in the appendices of this filing guide.

h. The proposed name is entered into our computer system to search for active corporations, limited liability companies and limited partnerships with phonetically similar names. The computer will produce a list of up to 72 entities with similar names. The document examiner then decides whether the proposed name is the same as, deceptively similar to, or similar to that of an existing entity.

i. Issuance of a certificate of incorporation does not authorize the use of a corporate name in this state in violation of the rights of another under the federal Trademark Act of 1946, the Texas trademark law, the Assumed Business or Professional Name Act, or the common law.

2. Duration

The duration of the corporation may be perpetual, a term of years, or a date certain.

3. Purpose

a. The TBCA, article 2.01, allows a corporation to be organized for any lawful purpose or purposes. The statement of purpose in the articles of incorporation may read as follows: "to transact any and all lawful business for which corporations may be organized under the Texas Business Corporation Act." Exception - The State Board of Insurance requires corporations seeking a license as an insurance agent to state a specific purpose to act as a specified type or types of insurance agents.

b. Corporations created for the purpose of operating non-profit institutions may not be formed as business corporations.

c. Business corporations may not engage in operating any of the following:
    (1) banks;
    (2) trust companies;
    (3) building and loan associations;
    (4) insurance companies;

(5) railroad companies;
(6) cemetery companies;
(7) cooperatives;
(8) labor unions; or
(9) abstract and title insurance companies.

d. Business corporations may not engage in activities for which a license is required, and such license cannot lawfully be granted to a corporation. Such activities are considered professional services for which professional corporations or associations may be formed.

Architects and engineers form business corporations rather than professional corporations. See Texas Attorney General Opinion Nos. M-539 and M-551, issued in 1970. Insurance agents may form either business or professional corporations. See Attorney General Opinion MW-99, issued in 1979.

e. Common mistakes in purpose clauses include:
(1) stating a power or purpose to act as trustee (trust company);
(2) stating a purpose to write bail bonds (insurance);
(3) stating a purpose to be general insurance agent. You should state a purpose to act as a particular type of agent covered by the Insurance Code, provided that such agent's license may be issued to a corporation;
(4) stating a purpose of accounting or auditing (a business corporation cannot be licensed by the Texas State Board of Public Accountancy).

4. Capital Stock

a. The articles of incorporation must include the aggregate number of shares the corporation is authorized to issue and their par value, or indicate that the shares are without par value or have no par value. Do not state that the par value is zero when you mean to designate that the shares have no par value.

b. If the shares are to be divided into classes, the articles of incorporation must state the number of shares in each class and the par value of each class. The preferences, limitations, and relative rights of each class must be included in the articles of incorporation.

c. Shares of any class may be issued in series if the articles of incorporation so provide. The series may be fixed in the articles of incorporation or designated by resolution of the board of directors if the articles of incorporation expressly vest authority in the board of directors to establish the series and determine the variations in the preferences, limitations and relative rights between series.

5. Commencement of Business

The articles must state that the corporation will not commence business until it has received for the issuance of shares consideration of the value of a stated sum, which shall be at least one thousand dollars ($1,000.00).

6. Registered Office/Agent

a. Every corporation is required to continuously maintain a registered agent and office for the purposes of service of process.

b. The articles of incorporation must include the street or building address of the registered office and the name of the registered agent at that address.

c. A post office box alone is not a sufficient address for the registered office.

d. If the registered office is in a city with a population of less than 5,000, the secretary of state will accept an address other than a street address for the registered office.

■ Whitewater Golf Business Plan

e. The registered agent may be a natural person, a Texas corporation, or a foreign corporation qualified to do business in Texas. A corporation may not serve as its own registered agent. Only one registered agent may be named in the articles of incorporation.

f. The business address of the registered agent must be the same as the registered office.

g. Clearly identify the address and name of the agent as that of the registered office and agent.

7. Directors

a. The articles of incorporation must state the number of directors constituting the initial board of directors and their names and addresses.

b. Only one director is required for a business corporation.

c. City and state are a sufficient address for the directors.

d. If the corporation is a close corporation not managed by a board of directors, the articles should set forth the names and addresses of the person or persons who, pursuant to the shareholders' agreement, will perform the function of the initial board of directors.

8. Incorporators

a. The articles should state the name and address of each incorporator.

b. City and state are a sufficient address for the incorporators.

c. Only one corporator is required, but every person who is listed as an incorporator must sign the documents.

d. Any natural person 18 or older, or any partnership, corporation, association, trust, or estate may serve as an incorporator.

e. There are no residency requirements for incorporators.

f. The function of the incorporator is to sign the articles of incorporation and deliver the documents to the secretary of state.

Execution Requirements and Fee

1. The articles should be signed by all the incorporators.

2. The Texas Business Corporation Act, article 10.02, provides that if a person signs a document which the person knows is false in any material respect with the intent that the document be delivered to the secretary of state to be filed on behalf of a corporation, the person has committed an offense. The offense is a Class A misdemeanor.

3. Two copies of the articles should be submitted to the secretary of state.

4. The filing fee is $300.00.

Common Errors Causing Rejection of a Proposed Filing

Most errors made in submitting articles of incorporation are procedural rather than substantive. Common errors include: failure to properly execute the documents; and failure to submit the proper fee.

Optional Provisions

The secretary of state does not review any of the optional provisions which may be included in the articles of incorporation. Optional provisions include:

(1) limiting or denying preemptive rights of the shareholders, TBCA, article 2.22-1;
(2) denying cumulative voting, TBCA, article 2.29;
(3) close corporation provisions, TBCA, Part Twelve;
(4) restriction on transfer of shares, TBCA, article 2.22E; and
(5) limiting director liability, Miscellaneous Corporation Laws Act, article 1302-7.06.

Procedures Prior To Filing

1. Name availability may be checked prior to submission of the articles by calling (512) 463-5555. A preliminary opinion is given on the availability of the proposed name. The final decision, however, is not made on the name until a document is submitted for filing. Do not advise your client to spend money or enter into contracts based on preliminary clearance of a name.

2. If pre-clearance of a name is obtained by telephone, a name reservation may be submitted to hold the name pending submission of the articles. The filing fee for the reservation is $40. The name is held for a 120 day period.

3. The secretary of state is checking a proposed corporate name only against other corporate, limited liability company and limited partnership names. It may be necessary to review state and federal trademark filings, and assumed name certificates filed with the county or the secretary of state to rule out the possibility of common law name infringement. Issuance of a certificate of incorporation does not authorize the use of a corporate name in this state in violation of the rights of another under the federal Trademark Act of 1946, the Texas trademark law, the Assumed Business or Professional Name Act, or the common law.

B U S I N E S S   P L A N   F O R

PD &M | Product Development & Marketing Co.

Patrick D. Holiday
Product Development & Marketing Co.
4601 North 19th Street, Suite A36A
Waco, Texas 76708

Source: Used by permission of P.D. (Pat) Holiday, Product Development & Marketing Co. in cooperation with The Business Resource Center, Waco, TX.

■ Product Development & Marketing Co. Business Plan

TABLE OF CONTENTS

Executive Summary

A. General Summary

Product Development & Marketing Co. (PD&M) is a consulting firm that assists inventors, entrepreneurs, and small businesses. With an emphasis on marketing, we offer our clients a commitment that includes prospecting for ideas, product development, market research, and assistance in obtaining patents or preparing a business plan. We also offer assistance with strategic planning, business expansion plans, and special projects. **At PD&M we are committed to getting your product/service successfully to the market.**

Our primary market is the Waco-McLennan County metropolitan area. Within the next three years we plan to expand to cities such as Temple, Killeen, Bryan College Station, Hillsboro, and Mexia.

At this time there are no other firms offering these services in the Waco area. This is advantageous from a marketing and promotion viewpoint, since most of our potential clients prefer to work with local businesses.

The focus of PD&M during early development is on assisting inventors and entrepreneurs. Long range plans are to include small businesses in the Waco metropolitan area with an emphasis on strategic planning, market research, business expansion plans, and special projects.

B. Resource Requirements

Initially, no outside financing is required. The owner's investment of $10,000 will cover the capital required for the start-up phase.

Description of Business

A. Company Objectives

Product Development & Marketing Company offers marketing services to inventors, entrepreneurs, and small businesses. Our principal service for inventors includes protecting their ideas and then proceeding with development and marketing. In essence, **all necessary services are made available to get an inventor's product or service successfully to market.** Our principal service for entrepreneurs encompasses product development, determining the "cost of goods," writing business plans, market research, and assistance in obtaining capital. Small businesses will receive assistance in areas such as writing business expansion plans, new product introduction, telemarketing, market research, and marketing strategy.

Initially, Product Development & Marketing Co. was organized as a sole proprietorship. Plans for incorporation in the near future may be forthcoming, depending on legal and tax advantages.

Every client has a unique product, service, or need. As a result every solution should be tailored to the customer, and this presents interesting challenges. I find this type of work to be very interesting and rewarding. I also enjoy working with inventors and marketing people. With my educational background, business experience, success in marketing, and adequate cash flow there is an excellent chance of success. It is the type of business that would be a natural for me to pursue.

To launch this business successfully, a working knowledge of patent law, trademarks, and copyrights is needed. It will also be necessary to generate interest and local support for this type of service. If necessary, I have plans to expand the customer base outside McLennan County and include key cities such as Temple as well as other large cities in Bell County.

In order for this business to be profitable, it will be necessary to draw adequate clientele and to organize most of the routine work for processing by people trained in this type of business. This can be accomplished by continual modernization of our methods and systems, and will require emphasis in the areas of training, special computer software, and market research.

■ Product Development & Marketing Co. Business Plan

B. Product/Service
The following is a breakdown, by client group, of the services PD&M provides:

Inventors
>   Document Disclosure
>   Inventor's Journal
>   Product Development
>   Patent Search
>   Patentability Opinion
>   Patent Application
>   Market Research
>   Manufacturing Sourcing
>   Market Invention (Technology Transfer)

Entrepreneurs
>   Market Research
>   Business Plans
>   Product Development

Businesses
>   Market Research
>   Strategic Planning
>   Telemarketing
>   Product Development
>   Sales Support
>   State-of-the-Art Patent Search
>   Special Projects
>   Business

Business Expansion Plans
Our services are important to inventors because of their need to protect their intellectual property (invention). We do this through the patent process. The typical patent process includes a Disclosure Document or Inventor's Journal, Patent Search with a Patentability Opinion from a registered patent attorney and finally a patent application. Once protected, the idea needs to be developed and made ready to market. The most common practice is to **license the product on a royalty basis.** Entrepreneurs have the need for market research, business plans, and venture capital. In order to remain competitive, companies need to constantly improve and/or add to their product line. This may require product development, market research, market planning, and business expansion plans. In some cases, an alternative is to locate a patent for a business that is compatible with their product line and market strategy. This is a very cost effective way product extension to increase sales and profit for a business.

Our business structure is inherently stable, since intellectual property is governed by patent law. Although there will be some changes required, these changes will come along with the need to develop patent law that is internationally focused as opposed to unique in the U.S.A. and each country. Marketing is an extremely dynamic field, and constant reading and information gathering will be required to stay current and abreast of the changes.

This type of consulting service does not require licensing or approval from state agencies. We will apply for company trademarks and copyrights in the future as may be deemed appropriate for PD&M Co. No patents or royalty agreements are involved during the initial startup phase.

C. Product/Service Development Plans
Most of the critical areas of the business will be developed and operational when we start business. Additional forms, procedures and many refinements will be developed and implemented during the first six months. These will be added to and enhanced substantially during the first two years. Resources such as *How To Make Money In Your Own Business* by E. Joseph Cossman, *Start Your Own Consulting Business* by James S. Pepitone, *The Inventor's Desktop Companion* by Richard C. Levy, and *Patent It Yourself* by David Pressman will be used. We also plan to investigate networking with other invention marketing companies. This will be beneficial to PD&M and our clients as well.

As with most businesses today, the need exists for conscious awareness of potential legal implications. There are many areas in which legal opinion would be desirable. It is impractical to have a lawyer on staff or to consult an attorney on every issue. However, the book *Patent It Yourself* by David Pressman is excellent and will be very helpful. An additional resource will be information by other firms along with forms and guidelines from the U.S. Government Printing Office.

Marketing

A. Market Analysis
Our market will include McLennan County and some towns outside this area. **Most of our customers will come from within a 30 mile driving distance.** We will also have occasional customers from cities such as Austin, Dallas, etc. Recently, there has been a trend for invention firms to expand nationally to increase their market.

Our primary customers will be inventors, entrepreneurs, and small businesses in the Waco metropolitan area. We also have an agreement to do engineering and development work, on a consulting basis, for the Speed Queen Co. in Ripon, Wisconsin. Our fastest growth will occur during the first three years as inventors hear about us and get to know about our services. With this foundation built, future growth will be based on increasing our market share and expanding beyond Waco into other major Texas cities. A potential market of 49 states is possible with national advertising. This will not be considered during the first 5 years.

Based on patent applications in the past two years there is a market potential of 2.4 clients per week from McLennan County alone. This can be doubled by including Bell County. Based on our initial staffing, it would be difficult to support a 10% market share, especially if we include all services.

In terms of **primary market research**, I spoke with Dr. Flynn Bucy of Baylor University and Chris Schmitz of the Waco Chamber of Commerce & Business Resource Center. Both indicated there is a need for this type service, especially in the area of marketing. I also discussed the need to assist entrepreneurs starting a new business with officers at M-Bank and Texas National Bank. Banks are now requiring business plans before a loan request is considered.

We feel it is important to offer all the services a client may need to get from the "idea stage" to obtaining a patent and successfully marketing the patent. No one provides this service in Waco, and no patent lawyers or patent agents serve in the Waco area. This is important, since most inventors prefer to work with local firms if the quality and cost of service is competitive.

B. Industry Analysis
One of the first patents in the U.S.A. was filed by Abraham Lincoln in 1849. Today, there are over 5 million patents filed at the U.S. Patent and Trademark Office. In recent years over 150,000 patent applications were filed per year with an approval rate exceeding 60%. Over 40% of these patents were issued to foreign countries.

There are approximately four national firms and one firm in Dallas that will compete for market share in the Waco area. The largest national firm is the Invention Submission Corp (ISC). They have been successful in attracting inventors but have not been effective in obtaining results. Kessler Sales Corp is a reputable firm that specializes in marketing inventions. They will attract a limited number of investors in this area. Synergy Consultants is the largest competitor, located in Dallas. This could turn out to be beneficial as we are looking at the possibility of networking together. The Affiliated Inventors Foundation, Inc. is located in Colorado and makes its services available to all states. Although Kessler Sales Corp and Affiliated Inventors Foundation, Inc. are formidable, they do not advertise extensively in the Waco area. Their services are also limited compared to what we are able to offer.

There are no national trade associations but there are many regional organizations that sponsor inventors' trade shows, lectures, and informative literature. The two largest annual trade shows offered for inventors are the Inventors Congress in California and New York. Many states have passed laws requiring marketing firms to provide their clients with information on their company when they offer their services. A typical requirement is to provide information on the percentage of clients receiving more money from their invention than they paid for the marketing service.

C. Customer Analysis
Our target customers are **inventors, entrepreneurs, and small business**. Our main customers during the first two years will be inventors.

Most inventors are skeptical and wary. They also lack the funds and skills necessary to develop and market their idea. A typical inventor has many ideas, is conceptual, and doesn't like paper work. Inventors will seek our service as they understand the need to protect their idea. Their main problem is lack of adequate funds to develop their idea in a complete and timely matter.

Entrepreneurs are also potential clients. Their average age is in the late 30's. Since many do not believe they need a business plan, they are more reluctant to secure our service. Many also lack funds to have a business plan professionally prepared. They usually secure this service as a result of the banker requiring a business plan prior to considering a loan request.

■ Product Development & Marketing Co. Business Plan

Most of our small business clients have a small staff and no marketing specialist. Small businesses will use our services to solve a current problem or to get a special project done on a timely basis without hiring additional help. We also offer experience, expertise, and objectivity that would not otherwise be available.

D. Competitive Analysis

As a result of my research, I have been able to estimate the competition's current market share, their strengths and their weaknesses. This information is recapped as follows:

Major Competitors	Market Share	Strengths	Weaknesses
ISC	40%	Marketing, Advertising	Credibility, Providing value to client, Expensive
Synergy Consultants	25%	Advertising, Located in TX	Expensive
Kessler Sales Corp	10%	Marketing of inventions	Lack of total service
Affiliated Inventors Corp.	5%	Inexpensive	No personal attention
Other Nat'l Firms	20%	Marketing, Advertising	Creditability, Providing value to client, Expensive

Since Product Development & Marketing Co. is a local company, I can take advantage of my reputation and use local advertising to reach my primary market. Clients from the Waco area will come to my office and I will have the opportunity to meet them and work with them on a personal basis. It should be noted their primary need is typically marketing, which is our strength. I also plan to conduct inventors' seminars and teach at McLennan Community College. Successful exposure will provide a basis for referrals through "word of mouth" advertising.

E. Advertising and Promotion

Our primary plans for advertising include the **yellow pages, invention magazines**, radio, and newspaper. I plan to conduct inventors' seminars, accept speaking engagements at various society meetings, and attend trade shows. Other possibilities include networking with firms like Synergy Consultants and obtaining clients through "word of mouth" advertising. I plan to conduct an average of 2-4 inventors' seminars per year. Our advertising budget will be over 10% of the first year and 6% of sales the following 2-3 years. Advertising will be based on response. Our fees are competitive and based on the amount of time and expense normally required to provide a specific service. A fee schedule is in the appendix. Special projects will be quoted on an estimated time and expense basis. We are estimating our sales to be $40,000 the first year and increasing at an average of 10-20% per year the following three years.

Strategic Planning

A. Long Term Goals

During our first three years we intend to fully develop our service for inventors while at the same time establishing a networking relationship with similar companies. We also plan to expand into large cities like Temple, Marlin, Hillsboro, and Killeen. We will investigate the possibility of introducing a special course for inventors at colleges and universities offering continuing education.

During the second and third year I plan to develop and introduce a specialized direct mail system to promote a **marketing service for small business.** This is the basic marketing plan for consultants as outlined in *Start Your Own Consulting Business* by James Pepitone.

The remaining two years of our five year plan will include additional emphasis on inventors' seminars and possible classes at colleges, as well as the expansion of our marketing services to small businesses. Additional skilled help and possibly an associate will be added as needed. We will also experiment with the possibility of actively pursuing clientele from surrounding cities such as Austin and Waxahachie while limiting the distance to less than 100 miles from Waco.

B. Critical Risks and Problems

It is important to develop an adequate clientele, but the main concern is developing a clientele base that can afford our professional services. Without this it would be impossible to make a reasonable profit.

Another concern is the cost of Errors and Omissions (E&O) liability insurance. This type of insurance is difficult to obtain and the cost is excessive when available. Currently the minimum cost is $5,000 per year. We will investigate insurance and incorporating as an alternative.

Although the time frame for receiving a financial return is long, **our greatest profit potential would come through royalties** we would receive in licensing (marketing) patents for our clients. This work includes negotiating a licensing agreement between our client and a manufacturer who is interested in licensing the patent and paying a royalty. We will also place emphasis on working with small business in the area of primary and secondary marketing research. This is a much needed and potentially profitable service.

Management & Organization

A. Key Management

P.D. (Pat) Holiday is manager and owner of Product Development and Marketing Co. He has a bachelor of Electrical Engineering degree with 5 years of staff management, 17 years of manufacturing experience including sales and marketing, and 8 years as president and CEO of Holiday-Hammond Corp. While at Holiday-Hammond Corp., he developed two new commercial dryers while adding various product improvements to the existing dryer line. While at Holiday-Hammond Corp. Pat was responsible for increasing the distributor network from 1 to 76 distributors, including 4 international distributors. Holiday-Hammond Corp. also expanded into the business of custom metal fabrication. This allowed HHC to take advantage of employee skills and the excess equipment capacity available. A resume is included in the Appendix.

Operations

A. Location Decision Factors

Initially PD&M will locate at the Business Resource Center. This is a new venture sponsored by the city of Waco, Baylor University, and MCC. Networking through the Business Resource Center will provide a mutually beneficial relationship. It is a natural place to obtain clients although most of the clientele coming to the Business Resource Center are there to visit the Small Business Development Center (SBDC). However, many of these clientele can use the professional services I provide. The visibility is not good but I would not expect many "walk-in" customers. The cost for space and services are reasonable at the Business Resource Center and it should be an excellent place to network with other businesses.

B. Regulatory Issues

We will be using a legal firm in Virginia to conduct our patent searches and file our patent applications. For this reason, it will not be necessary to have any permits or to be registered with the state or federal government. We have filed and registered with the county and state as a sole proprietorship. In the near future, we will consider incorporating.

■ Product Development & Marketing Co. Business Plan

Financial Information

A. Use Of Funds

Initially, no outside financing is required. The owner's investment of $10,000 will provide adequate capital to purchase the necessary office furniture, computer equipment, forms, and promotional materials and provide for adequate cash flow. A PD&M pro forma income statement, cash flow analysis, and balance sheet follow.

Product Development & Marketing Co.: Pro Forma Monthly Income Statement 1994

	Jan-94	Feb-94	Mar-94	Apr-94	May-94	Jun-94	Jul-94	Aug-94	Sep-94	Oct-94	Nov-94	Dec-94
Revenues	$1,500	$1,800	$2,200	$2,600	$3,000	$3,400	$3,800	$4,200	$4,500	$4,800	$4,300	$3,900
Sales allowances	$0	$0	$0	$0	$0	$0	$0	$0	$0	$0	$0	$0
Net Revenues	$1,500	$1,800	$2,200	$2,600	$3,000	$3,400	$3,800	$4,200	$4,500	$4,800	$4,300	$3,900
Cost of goods sold	$75	$90	$110	$130	$150	$170	$190	$210	$225	$240	$215	$195
Gross Margin	$1,425	$1,710	$2,090	$2,470	$2,850	$3,230	$3,610	$3,990	$4,275	$4,560	$4,085	$3,705
Expenses												
Selling												
Salaries	$0	$0	$0	$0	$0	$0	$0	$0	$0	$0	$0	$0
Advertising	$1,000	$800	$600	$250	$0	$250	$0	$250	$500	$250	$250	$0
Other	$125	$140	$160	$180	$200	$220	$240	$260	$275	$290	$265	$245
Total selling expens	$1,125	$940	$760	$430	$200	$470	$240	$510	$775	$540	$515	$245
General/Administrative												
Salaries	$250	$250	$250	$750	$950	$1,275	$1,275	$1,475	$1,475	$1,675	$1,675	$1,775
Employee benefits	$30	$30	$30	$90	$114	$153	$153	$177	$177	$201	$201	$213
Legal & Acctg.	$400	$300	$50	$50	$50	$50	$50	$50	$50	$50	$50	$50
Rent	$275	$275	$275	$275	$275	$275	$275	$275	$275	$275	$275	$275
Insurance	$300	$300	$300	$300	$300	$300	$300	$300	$300	$300	$300	$300
Depreciation	$50	$50	$50	$50	$50	$50	$50	$50	$50	$50	$50	$50
Telephone	$125	$125	$125	$125	$125	$125	$125	$125	$125	$125	$125	$125
Office supplies	$250	$50	$50	$50	$50	$50	$50	$50	$50	$50	$50	$50
Interest	$0	$0	$0	$0	$0	$0	$0	$0	$0	$0	$0	$0
Utilities	$0	$0	$0	$0	$0	$0	$0	$0	$0	$0	$0	$0
Bad debts	$33	$25	$25	$25	$25	$25	$25	$25	$25	$25	$25	$25
Other	$150	$100	$75	$75	$75	$75	$75	$75	$75	$75	$75	$75
Total G/A	$1,863	$1,505	$1,230	$1,790	$2,014	$2,378	$2,378	$2,602	$2,602	$2,826	$2,826	$2,938
TOTAL EXPENSES	$2,988	$2,445	$1,990	$2,220	$2,214	$2,848	$2,618	$3,112	$3,377	$3,366	$3,341	$3,183
N. Inc. before Taxes	($1,563)	($735)	$100	$250	$636	$382	$992	$878	$898	$1,194	$744	$522

Product Development & Marketing Co.: Pro Forma Monthly Cash Flow Statement
Starting Jan 1, 1994

	Jan-94	Feb-94	Mar-94	Apr-94	May-94	Jun-94	Jul-94	Aug-94	Sep-94	Oct-94	Nov-94	Dec-94
Receipts												
Cash sales	$0	$1,500	$1,800	$2.200	$2,600	$3,000	$3,400	$3,800	$4,200	$4,500	$4,800	$4,300
Loans	$0	$0	$0	$0	$0	$0	$0	$0	$0	$0	$0	$0
Owner's Injection	$10,000	$0	$0	$0	$0	$0	$0	$0	$0	$0	$0	$0
Total Receipts	$10,000	$1,500	$1,800	$2,200	$2,600	$3,000	$3,400	$3,800	$4,200	$4,500	$4,800	$4,300
Disbursements												
Direct materials	$75	$90	$110	$130	$150	$170	$190	$210	$225	$240	$215	$195
Direct labor	$0	$0	$0	$0	$0	$0	$0	$0	$0	$0	$0	$0
Equipment	$5,000	$0	$0	$0	$0	$0	$0	$0	$0	$0	$0	$0
Salaries	$250	$250	$250	$750	$950	$1,275	$1,275	$1,475	$1,475	$1,675	$1,675	$1,775
Rent	$275	$275	$275	$275	$275	$275	$275	$275	$275	$275	$275	$275
Insurance	$300	$300	$300	$300	$300	$300	$300	$300	$300	$300	$300	$300
Advertising	$1,000	$800	$600	$250	$0	$250	$0	$250	$500	$250	$250	$0
Taxes	$0	$0	$0	$441	$0	$441	$0	$0	$441	$0	$0	$441
Loan payments	$0	$0	$0	$0	$0	$0	$0	$0	$0	$0	$0	$0
Other	$955	$620	$365	$445	$489	$548	$568	$612	$627	$666	$641	$633
Total disbursements	$7,855	$2,335	$1,900	$2,591	$2,164	$3,259	$2,608	$3,122	$3,843	$3,406	$3,356	$3,619
Total Cash Flow	$2,145	($835)	($100)	($391)	$436	($259)	$792	$678	$357	$1,094	$1,444	$681
Beginning balance	$0	$2,145	$1,310	$1,210	$819	$1,255	$997	$1,789	$2,467	$2,824	$3,918	$5,362
Ending Balance	$2,145	$1,310	$1,210	$819	$1,255	$997	$1,789	$2,467	$2,824	$3,918	$5,362	$6,044

■ Product Development & Marketing Co. Business Plan

Product Development & Marketing Co.: Pro Forma Yearly Income Statement

	1994	%	1995	%	1996	%	1997	%	1998	%
Revenues	$40,000		$45,600		$51,984		$59,262		$67,558	
Sales allowances	$0		$456		$520		$593		$676	
Net Revenues	$40,000	100.0%	$45,144	100.0%	$51,464	100.0%	$58,669	100.0%	$66,883	100.0%
Cost of goods sold	$2,000	5.0%	$2,250	5.0%	$2,531	4.9%	$2,848	4.9%	$3,204	4.8%
Gross Margin	$38,000	95.0%	$42,894	95.0%	$48,933	95.1%	$55,821	95.1%	$63,679	95.2%
Expenses										
Selling										
Salaries	$0	0.0%	$0	0.0%	$0	0.0%	$0	0.0%	$0	0.0%
Advertising	$4,150	10.4%	$4,773	10.6%	$5,488	10.7%	$6,312	10.8%	$7,258	10.9%
Other	$2,600	6.5%	$2,990	6.6%	$3,439	6.7%	$3,954	6.7%	$4,547	6.8%
Total selling expenses	$6,750	16.9%	$7,763	17.2%	$8,927	17.3%	$10,266	17.5%	$11,806	17.7%
General/Administrative										
Salaries	$13,075	32.7%	$14,383	31.9%	$15,821	30.7%	$17,403	29.7%	$19,143	28.6%
Employee benefits	$1,569	3.9%	$1,765	3.9%	$1,986	3.9%	$2,234	3.8%	$2,513	3.8%
Professional services	$1,200	3.0%	$1,260	2.8%	$1,323	2.6%	$1,389	2.4%	$1,459	2.2%
Rent	$3,300	8.3%	$3,548	7.9%	$3,814	7.4%	$4,100	7.0%	$4,407	6.6%
Insurance	$3,600	9.0%	$3,960	8.8%	$4,356	8.5%	$4,792	8.2%	$5,271	7.9%
Depreciation	$600	1.5%	$675	1.5%	$759	1.5%	$854	1.5%	$961	1.4%
Amortization	$1,500	3.8%	$1,688	3.7%	$1,898	3.7%	$2,136	3.6%	$2,403	3.6%
Office supplies	$800	2.0%	$880	1.9%	$968	1.9%	$1,065	1.8%	$1,171	1.8%
Interest	$0	0.0%	$0	0.0%	$0	0.0%	$0	0.0%	$0	0.0%
Utilities	$0	0.0%	$0	0.0%	$0	0.0%	$0	0.0%	$0	0.0%
Bad debts/doubtful accounts	$308	0.8%	$355	0.8%	$408	0.8%	$469	0.8%	$539	0.8%
Other	$1,000	2.5%	$1,150	2.5%	$1,323	2.6%	$1,521	2.6%	$1,749	2.6%
Total G/A	$26,952	67.4%	$29,662	65.7%	$32,655	63.5%	$35,962	61.3%	$39,616	59.2%
TOTAL EXPENSES	$33,702	84.3%	$37,425	82.9%	$41,582	80.8%	$46,228	78.8%	$51,422	76.9%
N. Inc. before Taxes	$4,298	10.7%	$5,469	12.1%	$7,351	14.3%	$9,594	16.4%	$12,257	18.3%
Provision for taxes	$1,762	4.4%	$2,242	5.0%	$3,014	5.9%	$3,933	6.7%	$5,025	7.5%
Net Income after taxes	$2,536	6.3%	$3,227	7.1%	$4,337	8.4%	$5,660	9.6%	$7,232	10.8%
Prior period adjustment	$0	0.0%	$0	0.0%	$0	0.0%	$0	0.0%	$0	0.0%
Net Increase/(Decrease) to Retain	$2,536	6.3%	$3,227	7.1%	$4,337	8.4%	$5,660	9.6%	$7,232	10.8%

Product Development & Marketing Co.: Actual Balance Sheet
Year Starting Jan. 1, 1994

ASSETS			LIABILITIES	
Current Assets			Current Liabilities	
Cash		$10,000	Accounts Payable	$0
Accounts Receivable		0	Short-term Notes	$0
Less allowance for			Current Portion	
doubtful accounts	$0		of Long-term Debt	$0
Net realizable value		$0	Interest Payable	$0
Inventory		$0	Taxes Payable	$0
Temporary Investments		$0	Accrued Payroll	$0
Prepaid Expenses		$0	Total Current Liabilities	$0
Total Current Assets		$10,000		
			Long-term Liabilitites	$0
Long-term Investments		$0		
			Equity	
Fixed Assets			[Form depends on	
Land		$0	type of business	
Buildings $0 at			establishment.	
Cost, less accumulated				
depreciation of $0			A proprietorship	
Net book value		$0	lists owner's equity	
Equipment $0 at				
Cost, less accumulated			A partnership	
depreciation of $0			lists each partner's	
Net book value		$0	and total partners'	
Furniture/fixtures $0 at			equity.	
Cost, less accumulated				
depreciation of $0			A corporation	
Net book value		$0	shows capital stock,	
			paid-in capital,	
Total Net Fixed Assets		$0	etc.]	$10,000
Other Assets		$0		
			TOTAL LIABILITIES	
TOTAL ASSETS		**$10,000**	**AND EQUITY**	**$10,000**

■ Product Development & Marketing Co. Business Plan

Product Development & Marketing Co.: Pro Forma Balance Sheet
Year Ending Dec. 31, 1994

ASSETS			LIABILITIES		
Current Assets			**Current Liabilities**		
Cash		$522	Accounts Payable		$2,550
Accounts receivable	$3,900		Short-term Notes		$0
Less Allowance for			Current Portion		
doubtful accounts	$25		of long-term Debt		$0
Net realizable value		$3,875	Interest Payable		$0
Inventory		$0	Taxes Payable		$146
Temporary Investments		$0	Accrued Payroll		$900
Prepaid Expenses		$225	Total Current Liabilities		$3,596
Total Current Assets		$4,622			
			Long-term Liabilities		$0
Long-term Investments		$0			
			Equity		
Fixed Assets			[Form depends on		
Land		$0	type of business		
Buildings $0 at			establishment.		
Cost, less accumulated					
depreciation of $0			A proprietorship		
Net book value		$0	lists owner's equity.		
Equipment $0 at					
Cost, less accumulated			A partnership		
depreciation of $0			lists each partner's		
Net book value		$0	and total partners'		
Furniture/fixtures $5,000 at			equity.		
Cost, less accumulated					
depreciation of	$625		A corporation		
Net book value		$4,375	shows capital stock,		
			paid-in capital,		
Total Net Fixed Assets		$4,375	etc.]		$5,401
Other Assets		$0			
TOTAL ASSETS		**$8,997**	**TOTAL LIABILITIES AND EQUITY**		**$8,997**

Appendices and Exhibits

■ Product Development & Marketing Co. Business Plan

PATRICK D. HOLIDAY
808 Cardinal Drive
Waco, TX 76712
(817) 776-XXXX Hm
(817) 756-XXXX Wk

EDUCATION

University of Minnesota	B.E.E., June 12, 1965 5 year degree in Electrical Engineering with a minor in Industrial Engineering/Management
McLennan Community College	Various College courses in advertising, marketing, business, and computers.

EXPERIENCE

1988-Present   *Community College Instructor*

1979-1988   *Holiday-Hammond Corporation, Inc. — President/CEO*

Manufactured and distributed commercial dryers to the hotel/motel industry, the health care industry, and various other industries. During this time, two new dryers were developed and marketed. Our distributor network was increased from 1 national distributor in 1979 to 76 world-wide distributors in 1988. In 1988, the company was sold to Speed Queen Company.

1973-1979   *Eco Lab, Inc. — Plant Manager*

Responsible for manufacturing and quality of commercial washer and dryer production in Waco, TX. Production increased from an average of 10 units per month to over 150 units per month at peak production. Substantial improvements in quality were realized.

PROFESSIONAL ASSOCIATIONS

Society of Mechanical Engineers (SME)

Institute of Electrical and Electronic Engineers (IEEE)

MILITARY SERVICE

U.S. Air Force, Honorable Discharge

REFERENCES

Available upon Request

Fee Schedule

1. **Preliminary Appraisal:** We review your goals and discuss how they can be obtained and where PD&M can be of service. You choose the services you need. NO CHARGE for first visit.

2. **Invention Evaluation:** $95 – Over 30 areas are evaluated objectively to determine potential for commercial success. Evaluation includes recommendations on how to license your invention to industry.

3. **Disclosure Document:** $39

4. **Inventor's Journal:** $39 – Includes information with a sample entry to assist you in making your first entry, twelve suggestions for keeping a ledger, and "statements" to use for witness, notary, and drawings.

5. **Patent Search:** $350. This fee includes copies of patents (prior art) that are similar to your invention. This fee also includes a written opinion as to the patentability of your invention from a registered patent attorney.

6. **Start Up Package:** $495 – Includes: Invention Evaluation, Disclosure Document, Drawings, Inventor's Journal, Patent Search, and Patent Opinion.

7. **Patent Application, Preparation and Filing:** Utility Patents ($2,000 for typical mechanical patent application.) A quote will be furnished on complicated or involved patents.
Design Patents – $650

8. **Copyright:** $25 to fill out application – ready for your signature and submittal.

9. **Trademark:** $45 to fill out application. Trademark Search (all 50 states and federal registers) = $195, Drawing = $100 (typical)

10. **Engineering Services:** Estimates are provided on NO CHARGE basis. We can work with you on an hourly rate or on a quoted fee based on the work we are requested to do.

11. **Drafting:** Most of our drafting is done on a CAD (Computer Aided Drafting) System. Typical prices are:
    $30 – $50 for A size drawing
    $50 – $75 for B size drawing
    $75 – $150 for C size drawing
    A typical price for a drawing addition/correction is $10 – $20. If requested, an actual quote will be provided prior to starting work based on your sketch. A 5-1/4 inch diskette back-up can be provided for $5.

12. **Business Plan:** $650 – $1,900 depending on complexity, size of plan, and market research required.

13. **Market Research (Primary):** $475 – $1,250 for a simple market survey based on minimum sampling techniques. If more than 95% reliability is required, we suggest services such as A.C. Nielsen be considered.

14. **Target Company Search:** $395 – $675 to contact manufacturers of your type product and obtain information on potential marketability, possible interest, submittal policy, attitude, etc.

15. **Market Research (Focus-Group Study):** $1,950 for a small independent group. There is an additional charge for video tape and supplemental evaluators.

16. **Market Research (Secondary):** $100 – $1,000 depending on complexity and amount of market and/or demographics information needed.

17. **Marketing Assistance:** Assistance is provided in selling your invention and/or invention rights. A fee will be quoted based on the complexity and amount of involvement of Product Development and Marketing Co. This work can be done on an hourly basis or on a commission basis (typical rate is 25%). No fee is paid on a commission basis unless we are successful in selling or licensing the patent for the client.

18. **Seed Money Financing:** $995. This is a practical way to obtain seed money to get your idea developed, patented, and ready to market. It includes documents to incorporate, issue stock, corporate notes, and stock certificates, etc.

19. **Venture Capital:** This can be done on a fee basis or on a percentage basis (typical rate is 6 to 15%). No fee is paid on a commission basis unless we are successful in obtaining venture capital for the client.

NOTE: Prices are subject to change.

■ Product Development & Marketing Co. Business Plan

Inventors – Protect Your Idea

One of the greatest concerns an inventor has is protecting their idea. Product Development & Marketing Co. recommends the first step for every inventor is to record their idea. To accomplish this we recommend two alternatives. These are the **Inventor's Journal** and the **Disclosure Document.**

When choosing an **Inventor's Journal**, make sure that it is bound, lined, and the pages are numbered. After making your first (initial) entry describing your invention, it is recommended you have it witnessed and notarized. As you continue to work on your patent, make entries in the Inventor's Journal, sign and date them. It is also very important that you have each page witnessed. Approximately every six months you should have your Inventor's Journal notarized.

Recently the **Disclosure Document** has become a favorite way of recording the date of conception for an invention. This service is provided by the U.S. Patent and Trademark Office. Two copies of your invention with a cover letter are submitted as a Disclosure Document. They are both stamped with the same identification number and date of receipt. One of these copies is returned to you for future reference. Once the Disclosure Document is filed, you have the protection needed to develop your patent so application can be made. You have two years to apply for a patent. The Document Disclosure program does not take away from the value of a conventional witnessed and notarized Inventor's Journal that includes evidence as conception of an invention. The Document Disclosure program provides a credible form of evidence including registration with the U.S. Patent and Trademark Office.

CAUTION: It is recommended that one of the above alternatives be used in place of mailing a disclosure letter to oneself or another person by registered mail.

CAUTION: Any public use or sale in the United States or publication of your invention anywhere in the world more than one year prior to the filing of a patent application on your invention will prohibit the granting of your patent.

RECOMMENDATION: Product Development and Marketing Co. offers a full range of services and would appreciate the opportunity to work with you on your invention. An initial consultation is offered at **no charge**. We would like to work with you in preparing and submitting a Disclosure Document or Inventor's Journal. Our office has both of these available at $39 each which includes our assistance in filling them out. Once you have taken this step we are prepared to take you to the next phase of getting your product successfully to the market.

Confidentiality and Non-Use Statement

Product Development and Marketing Co. is in the business of assisting inventors and entrepreneurs in getting their product or service successfully to market. Our company's integrity depends on maintaining the confidentiality of all products and services presented to it.

Product Development and Marketing Co. and/or its agents agree the idea, invention, product, or service you are disclosing, and which you believe to be your own original creation, shall not be disclosed without your permission. Product Development and Marketing Co. also agrees that any changes, modifications, and/or improvements suggested or made by our company will automatically become your property.

Product Development and Marketing Co. cannot assume any responsibility with respect to features of the invention which can be demonstrated to be already known to us or rightfully belong to another inventor.

In consideration of the above, you have approached Product Development and Marketing Co. for the purpose of discussing your idea, product, or service known (described) as:

_____

to determine if the services offered by Product Development and Marketing Co. would be beneficial.

Agreed on this _____ day of _____ , 1994.

_____

P.D. (Pat) Holiday, President
Product Development & Marketing Co.

NOTE: This form is for your protection and should remain in your possession.